2nd EDITION

GRECO card LTD

editorial • tourist • advertising

3 Aglavrou str., Athens, Tel.: (01) 9248292 / 293, Fax: (01) 9241910

Publisher: Georgios Monemvasitis
Editor: Si Enorasis Advertising
Author: Eleni Daskalakis
Photography: Alexis Rodopoulos - The Society for
Turtle Protection
Colour Separations: APOPSIS
DTP: Si Enorasis Advertising
Printing Co-ordinator: LAITMER
Printing: S. NANOS S.A.
Binding: Th. Iliopoulos, P. Rodopoulos Ltd.
Translation: ALDI Ltd. - PROCESS.1.
ISBN 960-7436-24-5

Dear reader, the book in your possession is the direct result of great efforts by a large number of people who tried very hard to get to know the island of Zakynthos and understand the mentality of its inhabitants. For all of us who've worked hard for its creation and who've witnessed its writing page-for-page, this book is something very valuable, because it represents our desire to design a guide that we would like to have whenever we visit a new island.

This book involves a great deal of love and care for an island that is certain to impress every visitor.

Our goal has been to create a book that is a true companion and friend to every first-time visitor to Zakynthos, one that will take visitors by the hand through all its beauty and glorious past.

A guide that will take one to beautiful beaches, cosmopolitan villages, and give one the chance to experience the small pleasures that only Zakynthos can offer: the captivating sunset in Keri, the waters in the harbour as they gradually change colours, which can only been seen from Bochali, the great tavern in Schiza...

We thank all the island's inhabitants for making us feel so welcome, for talking to us, revealing their island's secrets, and for making us feel at home. Without their invaluable help we would have not been able to discover the true character of this unique part of the Ionian, the Fior di levante.

Enjoy yourself

careta
careta

TURTLES ON ZAKYNTHOS

For thousands of years, turtles have lived and laid their eggs in the Mediterranean. Thoughtless human intervention however, has placed these species in immediate danger of extinction, as egg-laying beaches are destroyed, an increasing number of turtles are trapped and perish in fishing nets and trawl-lines, and the seas are becoming increasingly polluted. This has led to the establishment of international laws for the protection of turtles, in most cases declared an endangered species.

One of these endangered species, the Caretta-Caretta turtle has chosen to lay its eggs on the shores along the island of Zakynthos. More so than in any other part in the Mediterranean, the Caretta-Caretta creates an average of 1.300 nests along six (6) beaches in the gulf of Laganas, about 5 kilometres long. The increasing international significance of the gulf of Laganas has encouraged the State to adopt a series of measures aimed at protecting the turtle's natural habitat, and is currently looking into the establishment of the National Marine Park of Zakynthos. Every summer, the Society for Turtle Protection arranges the scientific observation of these nests in association with various Ministries, volunteers and researchers from Greece and abroad.

Visitors to the island are kindly reminded that their contribution is vital to the survival of the Caretta-Caretta turtle and are encouraged to respect a few simple regulations that go a long way in ensuring the safety of their egg-laying habitats. Beaches along the gulf of Laganas should be vacated between sunset and sunrise, while the use of umbrellas and deck-chairs is strictly forbidden with the exception of specially designated areas. No speed boats are allowed within the bay at any time. The Society for Turtle Protection wishes to stress the importance of these few simple rules and reminds visitors to this beautiful island that both the survival of these turtles, the preservation of their natural habitat and the success of the National Marine Park depends on their co-operation.

More information regarding turtle protection is available from the Society's kiosks, on a number of beaches around the island, and through local authorities. Alternatively, one should contact the Society for Turtle Protection on 1 I. Plessa street, 29100 Zakynthos, or call 0695 - 28 658 (+ Fax).

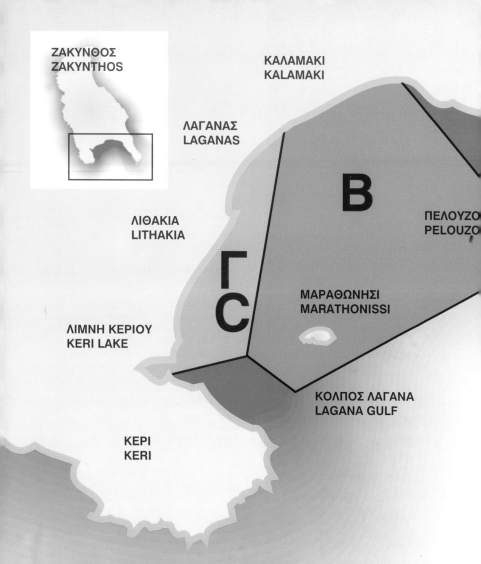

ΖΑΚΥΝΘΟΣ
ZAKYNTHOS

ΚΑΛΑΜΑΚΙ
KALAMAKI

ΛΑΓΑΝΑΣ
LAGANAS

B

ΠΕΛΟΥΖΟ
PELOUZO

ΛΙΘΑΚΙΑ
LITHAKIA

Γ
C

ΜΑΡΑΘΩΝΗΣΙ
MARATHONISSI

ΛΙΜΝΗ ΚΕΡΙΟΥ
KERI LAKE

ΚΟΛΠΟΣ ΛΑΓΑΝΑ
LAGANA GULF

ΚΕΡΙ
KERI

ΑΣΙΛΙΚΟΣ
ASILIKOS

Α. ΓΕΡΑΚΙ
GERAKI CAPE

BOATING RESTRICTIONS IN THE BAY OF LAGANAS

The Bay of Laganas in Zakynthos is the most important nesting area for the loggerhead turtle (Caretta-caretta) in the Mediterranean. Apart from specific legislation (Presidential Decree of 5/7/90, Goverment Cazette 347/D) that has been enacted to protect the nesting beaches and a broader surrounding area, the Coast Guard of Zakynthos has issued two Local Port Regulation (Ref. Num. 19/91, and 20/94 Goverment Gazettes 585/B/91 & 598/B/94). According to these, the Bay is divided into three zones, in which the following laws are effective from 1 May through to 31 October each year.

MARITIME ZONE A:

It is forbidden for any boat or vessel to enter or moor within this zone. Fishing with any kind of fishing gear is prohibited.

MARITIME ZONE B:

It is forbidden for any boat or vessel to travel at a speed greater than 6 knots, and to moor or anchor within this zone.

MARITIME ZONE C:

It is forbidden for any boat or vessel to travel at a speed greater than 6 knots, within this zone.

CONTENTS

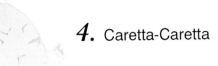

Introduction

ZAKYNTHOS
AT A GLANCE

Zakynthos, the third largest Ionian island after Kefallonia and Corfu, and the eleventh in size in Greece, is situated opposite the coast of the County of Ilia, on the Peloponnese, at a distance of 17 nautical miles from the shore and 14 nautical miles south of Kefallonia. Together with

Back in prehistoric times, Zakynthos was part of the area's seabed only to emerge after a powerful earthquake shook the area and created large rifts at the bottom of the sea. In fact, the sea across its south-eastern coast has the deepest point in the entire Mediterranean basin: the "Well of Oinouses" as it is known, measures about 4.500 metres deep.

Aghios Dionysios at sundown

the isles of Strofades, situated about 37 nautical miles south of Zakynthos, opposite the gulf of Kyparissia on the Peloponnese, they comprise the County of Zakynthos, which spans over an area of 406 square kilometres and has a population, according to a 1991 census, of 35.000 inhabitants.

NATURE...
THE COASTLINE

The earthquakes responsible for creating the island also caused a number of rocky barriers, reefs and many isles, the most significant of these being the group called Strofades. The geological changes caused by the earthquakes are responsible for the island's highly diversified coastal landscape, which features smooth sandy beaches along its north-eastern part and vertical, steep, and often rocky shores on its south-western side.

Zakynthos resembles an irregular triangle: the island's western coastline, from the northern cape of Skinari to the southern cape of Marathias, is 34 km long and steep, creating numerous caves and different: ideal for swimming, these beaches are smooth, sandy and generally peaceful, and stretch over a distance of 37 km. They begin from the cape of Skinari, the island's northernmost point, and run in a south-eastern direction all the way to cape Gerakas.

When touring the island by boat from Zakynthos town, Skinari is usually the point at which calm waters suddenly change into rough

The impressive caves in Keri

The famous Shipwreck

secluded coves. The island's most-photographed beach, the famous Shipwreck, which is flocked by thousands of tourists who come to see it for themselves and swim in its crystal clear waters every year, is located between these two points.

The island's coastline which is opposite the Peloponnese is very

seas, almost always surprising all passengers on board. The next "pleasant" surprise comes as the Blue Caves come into view and passengers are able to witness the colouring effects of the water on the rocks above. The caves that have been created along the island's rocky coastline are truly impressive, both in their shape and size as well as in the colour of their waters, and represent a strong pole of attraction for visitors. The most famous of these is the Blue Cave, which is near cape Skinari, in the northern part of the island (see tour No 6).

The bay of Laganas, which is one of Zakynthos' most touristy areas, is between the capes of Marathias and Gerakas. The bay includes the isles of Marathonisi and Pelouzi and its warm waters provide shelter to the Caretta-Caretta turtle, the island's symbol of ecology.

THE ISLAND'S INTERIOR
Most of the island's landscape is mountainous, the tallest of which is Mt. Vrachionas (758 m), in its western part, and Mt. Skopos (492 m), which stretches all the way to cape Gerakas. Zakynthos does not have large rivers: in fact, the only rivers are Ag. Charalambous, which runs through town, and Skourtis, a smaller one in Alykes. Across the island, however, one often drives past small streams and ravines. Zakynthos' landscape can be divided geographically and geologically into three sections, from north to south.

The first such section starts from cape Skinari and moves in a southern direction, occupying the western part of the island, up to the south-western cape of Marathias. This part of the island is the most scarcely populated and the coastline is mostly characterised by

steep rocky shores and breathtaking caves.

The island's middle section begins in the north, at the bay of Alykes, and ends at the bay of Laganas. This flat part features the fertile valley, where the island's inhabitants cultivate the vine that produces the island's tasty wine, and the town of Zakynthos. Most of the island's inhabitants live in Zakynthos town, about 10.000 people all together.

Old methods surviving to our days
The process of drying sultanas

A harmony of colours

The third section surrounds the eastern and south-eastern part of the island, all the way to cape Gerakas, and includes some of Zakynthos' most beautiful beaches. Zakynthos has been known from ancient times for its hot springs, the most famous of which are the following: Ag. Panteleimon in the municipality of Pigadakia, Vromoneri or Nera tou Kareri in the municipality of Kato Gerakari, a spring that is said to offer relief from rheumatism, Maghiorou Langadia in the municipality of Koukesi Kallitheas, a mineral water spring, and Tsouri in the municipality of Ag. Dimitrios, whose water is used as a cure for scabies, itchiness and arthritis. Other springs are Xyghia in the municipality of Orthonies, Tetartia in the village of Gerakari, Kolosourtis in the bay of Alykes, Magera and Gremina in the municipality of Skoulikados, and Dragonaras in the municipality of Ano Volimes.

It is worth mentioning the two springs in the harbour of Nafthis or Keriou that produce water with tar. One of the springs is called Herodotus' Well or Pigi tou Irodotou and local history relates it to the ancient Greek historian himself. Similar wells have been discovered in other parts of the island as well, but their great depth does not allow their exploitation for oil extraction purposes.

CLIMATE AND CROPS

The mild, Mediterranean climate, with significant rainfall and elevated humidity, transforms Zakynthos into a very green landscape, which blossoms in spring even in its most arid parts. The island's prevailing green colour inspired the Venetian who called it the "flower of the East", or "Fior di levante" in their language.

During summer, the temperature fluctuates - on average - around 27 C in August, while in winter it drops to about 11 C in January. Rainfall on the island is a significant aspect of its climate (average yearly rainfall about 984.5 millimetres), while the sight of the island covered in snow is quite rare. Winters are mild and summers are cool, a combination which favours the cultivation of sensitive crops such as vine, olives, garden produce and citrus fruits. From the old days, the most important occupation of the island's inhabitants was the cultivation of sultanas. To stress the importance of this crop in local trade, it used to be said that punishment by death should be attributed only to two types of criminals: traitors and sultana-smugglers!

The island's soil blesses local grapes with a particular flavour, which makes the local wine, "verdea", greatly sought after, particularly when accompanied by local oil-cheese. During summer, the season for onions, each grocery shop eagerly displays strings of the local large, sweet onions.

Bougarini, the perfume from Zakynthos, was very famous and is still found in shops around the island. Let us not forget powder production, which at some stage supported the island's economy, and the workshops that produce the best nougat and sesame-seed bars to our days.

...AND THE INHABITANTS

The people of Zakynthos are optimists, genial and friendly both towards their fellow islanders and to all the island's visitors. Famous for their jokes and the pranks they pull on eachother as well as on the inhabitants of other Ionian islands, Zakynthians are well known for their

The harvest is over

chatty nature and lively gestures. The local dialect is very song-like and many of the words used in the island's colloquial language have Italian roots. The islanders' great love of art, in its every form, is evident every step of the way, and it is no surprise that Zakynthos has given rise to many famous personalities both in dancing,

The island's constant struggle against the peculiarities of nature has yielded stubborn and strong inhabitants, who have succeeded in overcoming their fear of earthquakes and have always accepted the bitter consequences with great hope and self-confidence, certain that tomorrow will bring a better day!

Working with sultanas

literature, and arts in general. And there is no need to stress the islanders' inclination towards music, because this is quite obvious as soon as they begin to speak. Zakynthians love their island, their villages, the church and their saints. The islanders also have a great love for life, which they eagerly demonstrate in their gatherings and serenades, always accompanied by a glass of wine.

The island's geographical vicinity to the west has lent a degree of finesse and open-mindedness to all Zakynthians. Nature has gifted the island's inhabitants with a polite character and an innate instinct for hospitality. Even to our days, where hospitality has become a profession, the islanders' smile and welcomming nature comes straight from the heart.

History

Zakynthos was first mentioned in Homeric plays. According to Homer, the island got its name from Zakynthos, who was its first settler: Zakynthos, the son of Dardanos, king of Troy, arrived to the island from the Arcadian city of Psofida, around 1500-1600 BC, with his men. These first settlers fortified the island's acropolis and named it Psofida, to honour and remember their homeland. Another name for the island mentioned by Homer is Iliessa, which means "forested land". According to Plinios, before Zakynthos, the island was called Yria after its previous settler, the Arcadian hero Yrieas. This view claims that the island's first settlers came from the Peloponnese, although there is another view which believes that the name Yria comes from settlers that originated from Yria in Boeotia.

Many historians have expressed personal opinions regarding the origin of the island's name. Wood claims that the name derives from the words "Za" (which in ancient Greek means "many") and "Kythnos" (which means "hill"), and bases his view on the island's mountainous landscape. Other authors attribute a series of names to the island, such as: Diakynthos, Diakythos, Iakynthos, Zakita, Jacinthum, Jantes, Lesande etc. using as it would seem, certain variations of its present name.

ANCIENT TIMES

The history of Zakynthos, as is the case with the rest of the Ionian islands, has its roots well into antiquity. Times full of adventure, conquerors and besiegers, during which Zakynthos plays an important role in the region's historical and cultural development. Its inhabitants, closely acquainted with the mentality and civilisation of a series of European peoples, were able to borrow and assimilate their most notable characteristics, thereby moulding their own particular personality, safeguarding their Greek identity, and at the same time broadening their cultural and spiritual evolution.

The oldest signs of life on Zakynthos, dating back to Neolithic times, were discovered in the Gulf of Laganas. Fossilised bones dating back to Palaeolithic times were also discovered on the same shore.

Archaeological finds and scripts of ancient authors certify the blossoming of a significant civilisation on Zakynthos, substantial evidence of which however - possibly due to many devastating earthquakes - has yet to be discovered, which would create a more complete picture of the island's past.

A marble cluster was discovered at the site of the ancient acropolis of Zakynthos - close to the castle - which portrayed Apollo, Aphrodite and Artemis. The find is currently housed in the Tiembolo Museum in Venice. Coins dating back to ancient times, ruins of ancient temples and tombs have also been discovered on the island.

The Arcadians that followed
Zakynthos to the island,
entrenched themselves in their
new acropolis, made good use
of the island's rich and fertile
soil, developed wealth and
began establishing
communities. Their ships led
them to Spain where they
established a community
called Zakantha, which
blossomed both in wealth and
in terms of civilisation for over
or Paranassia on the Spanish
cape of Pirineo.
During the years that followed,
Zakynthos was reigned by
king Arkeisios of Kefallonia
and subsequently fell into the
hands of Ulysses, son of
Laertis, and later to the king
of Ithaka. The mythical slaying
of Penelope's wooers, among
whom also twenty
Zakynthians, was the reason
behind the decline of Ulysses'

A view of Zakynthos

one thousand years before
being destroyed by Hannibal
in 218 BC. Another Zakynthian
community was the town of
Kydonies on Crete, while there
was another community on
Paros and, together with the
Phocaeans, the Zakynthians
established the city of Fokida
domain.
The intervention of
Neptolemos saw the signing of
the treaty with which
Zakynthos, although no longer
under Ithaka's domain, was
nonetheless obliged to pay a
yearly tax. The most important
aspect of the treaty however,

was the fact that for the very first time in Greek history there appeared to be a right to self-determination and democratic governing of a certain region.

The democratic era on Zakynthos lasted some 650 years. Its geographical location, fertile soil and tar deposits helped its economic development. The first silver coin is mint around the 6th century BC and on its one side features Apollo's sacred symbol, the Tripod. Around succeeds in remaining neutral up to the battle of Plataea, during which, along with the Lacedaemonians, the Zakynthians pursue the Persians to Asia. The alliance between the Zakynthians and Lacedaemonians was interrupted by the Athenian commander, Tolmides, when he burnt down the Spartan arsenal in 455 BC. This event led the Zakynthians into alliance with the Athenians. When the Peloponnesian war broke out, Zakynthos stood by

A pre-earthquake photo of the port

the 5th century BC, the Tripod is replaced by the image of the god himself, holding a lyre.

During the course of the Persian Wars, Zakynthos the side of neighbouring Corfu during their conflict with the Corinthians - which was one of the causes of the war.

After the expedition to Sicily, which led to the overwhelming defeat of the Athenians, Zakynthos once again found itself under the domain of the Lacedaemonians, who altered the island's democratic statute into an oligarchy, according to their particular principles. The inhabitants, encouraged by a similar move led by Thrasyvoulos in Athens, revolted and restored democracy on the island. During the Macedon wars, the Zakynthians were unable to hold a neutral stance as they had done during the Persian Zakynthos passes under the domain of the roman commander Nevinio and then again under Philip's, until its final annexation to the roman province of Achaia.

ROMAN & BYZANTINE TIMES

During the historical period in which many Greek cities were under the domain of the Roman Empire, Zakynthos is subjected to the same fate as the rest of the Ionian islands. It seems that, from the very

A view of Zakynthos before the earthquake

wars previously, which resulted in the island being subjected to an interchange of Macedon and Roman conquerors. From the domain of Philip the 2nd, in 217 BC first time the Romans conquered the island, they realised its geographic and strategic importance for the expansion of their empire as well as its great wealth.

Around 146 BC, Zakynthos is included in the Roman Province of Achaia, which comprised Epirus, the Peloponnese and the islands, with the exception of Crete. During the first years of Roman dominion, Zakynthos was governed by Roman Pro-Consuls. Later the island was permitted to establish its own laws subject to paying a yearly tax and supplying men in aid of the roman army. The city had its own municipality, parliament, legislation, and coin with a separate emblem. This period of autonomy contributed significantly to the island's cultural development and became the visiting grounds for famous intellectuals from Rome. Zakynthos will loose these rights under the government of the Antonines' dynasty. During the Mithradatic wars the Zakynthians remain neutral, while many Greeks oppose the Roman Empire. But when the general of Mithradates, Archelaos, is defeated during his expedition to Greece in Haironia by the Consul Sulla, he sails to the Ionian and lays siege on Zakynthos. The Zakynthians barricade themselves in their acropolis and with the help of the Romans succeed in breaking the siege.

During that period, Christianity starts to spread in Zakynthos. There are two separate traditions regarding the first to preach Christianity on the island, none of which however have been historically proven. The first states that around 34 AD, Mary Magdalene and Mary, wife of Clopas, during their voyage to Rome, disembark on Zakynthos and become the first to preach Christianity on the island. The name of a village on the island's western side bears witness to this tradition: Maries, as it is called, stages a great yearly feast in honour of Mary Magdalene. The second tradition believes that Christianity reached the island through the preaching of Saint Beatrice, who advocated the word of Christ to local inhabitants.

The decline of the Roman Empire made the Ionian Sea and Zakynthos the pray of pirates and skilled conquerors. When Constantine the Great created the Byzantine Empire, Zakynthos belonged to the Province of Illyria. During those times, the Byzantine Empire was at its peak and while the Ionians expected to count on the help of the Empire to defend themselves against pirate attacks, the Byzantine were occupied with their internal affairs and were unable to come to their aid.

During Byzantine dominion, the island's inhabitants were divided into three social classes. The island's large landowners belonged to the social class of the "Decurions" or the "Illustrious", while labourers and tradesmen belonged to the second social class, and farmers belonged to the third.

Around 466 AD, Zakynthos is subjected to the fury of the king of the African Vandals, Guilderich, who conquered the island with his 60 ships. His

Past remains

men robbed and burnt the island's homes, raped and slaughtered its inhabitants. On his departure, Guilderich took 500 of the island's Illustrious as hostages and slaughtered them on his way to the Adriatic. Apart from numerous barbarian attacks, in 591 AD the island will also be subjected to the plague which has infested the entire Empire. During the Isavri Dynasty, the Byzantine Empire is divided into Prefectures. Zakynthos is excluded from the Province of Achaia and is incorporated into the 11th Prefecture of Longobard, whose capital was Ravenna in Italy, and later, around 887 AD, into the Prefecture of Kefallinia, which included all the Ionian islands. The characteristic of Byzantine Zakynthos was that it was subjected to the

Pre-earthquake photo of Solomoù square

administration of the Empire's western Regions. Over the next years, the Saracens lay siege and begin looting the island. With the intervention of the admirals Nikedas and Narses, the Zakynthians manage to rid themselves of the threat of the Saracens.

CRUSADES & FRANKISH RULE

Zakynthos' adventures, along with those of other Ionian islands, do not end here. Their past is a highly eventful one, as they form an important junction between East and West, and hence represent an invaluable piece of territory. During the Crusades, the island is once again subjected to severe looting and devastation. On his return from the 2nd Crusade, Boemundo the Norman savagely loots the Ionian islands. His rage is fuelled by his desire to avenge his father's failure, Giscard, to conquer the islands of Zakynthos and Kefallonia. During the 4th Crusade, Zakynthos finally succumbs to the Venetian, who annex it to the principality of Achaia, along with Kefallonia. At the end of the 12th century, Zakynthos passes under the domain of the Italian palatine counts of Orsini, who ruled the island until 1357. One of count Orsini's very first moves, in an effort to win the sympathy of the catholic clergy, is his letter addressed to the Roman Pope, Innocent the 3rd, in which he places the religious side of the island in the hands of the Pope. The orthodox bishop Agapios is

Old oil containers

expelled from the island and the clergy is forced to recognise the Pope's supremacy.

In 1357, the Orsini family offers the command of Zakynthos to its "son-in-law" Leonardo Tocco as a gift in matrimony to Roberto Orsini's sister, Francesca. This marked the start of the Tocco, or De Tocchi, dynasty on the island, who governed it for over a century, with the exception of a brief interval, during which Zakynthos fell to the Turkish Sultan. In 1452, Leonardo Tocco the 2nd, re-founded the Orthodox Bishopric of Kefallonia and Zakynthos, and restored the Orthodox Bishop, thereby satisfying public demand for religious freedom. However, in 1479 the last of the De Tocchi dynasty, Leonardo the 3rd, faced by the Turkish threat, decides within a night to flee to Italy and sell his property to subjects of the Venetian Democracy, abandoning the island once again to the command of the Venetian commissioner.

The attack that Leonardo Tocco feared was now imminent as the Turkish fleet was on the look-out. The island's inhabitants are spared at the very last minute when the Venetian admiral, Loredainus, happens to sail past Zakynthos with his fleet and comes up against Kapoudan Pasha, just as the latter is getting ready to attack the island, after looting Kefallonia. Negotiations with the Pasha succeed in granting Zakynthians and Venetian safe passage from the island to seek refuge on Venetian territory in the Peloponnese. Zakynthos did not avoid looting and devastation by the Turks, but this decision saved many human lives.

The Tocco dynasty, which governed the island for approximately one hundred years, had a few righteous fighter-family-members, who defended their territorial integrity and respected the lifestyle and belief of its local inhabitants. However, there were also other family members who were bellicose and greedy and who constantly put islanders' lives in danger. On the whole, however, the De Tocchi dynasty organised the island's administration and economy, providing its inhabitants with peace and stability. These favourable times also enabled the island's population to increase to 25.000 inhabitants. Some five years later, in 1485, the Venetian succeed to beat the Turks on a diplomatic scale and regain control of Zakynthos provided they pay 500 ducats yearly to the Sultan.

VENETIAN RULE & FRENCH DEMOCRATS

Once the fury of Kapudan Pasha died out, the Venetian took over the island and discovered a land devastated by looting and the destructive nature of the Turks. They concerned themselves immediately with the revival of the island and offered all those who wished to take up residence in Zakynthos, from territories under Venetian domain, significant privileges

A bell-tower defying the forces of nature

and tax exemptions. The aristocracy who commanded the island began to distribute land and homes to new arrivals who started to flock the island by the thousands. The families of Venetian aristocracy were given titles and great honours, and had their family names registered in the island's famous "Golden Bible", or Libro d'Oro.

suggest that, from the deserted land that it was in 1480, Zakynthos boasted some 20.000 inhabitants in less than twenty years time. This sudden increase in population was almost the cause of friction between the remaining inhabitants and newcomers. To avoid any conflict, in 1499 the Doge of Venice issued a decree which

The home of Dionysios Solomos

Honours and titles were also given to all those who offered their services to Venice, by guarding the island's coastline against the danger of pirate attacks.
Life was gradually restored on Zakynthos and a new era of development and reform was underway. Reliable sources

safeguarded the rights of the island's previous landowners. At the same time a large portion of the island's forests was allocated to farming. The two major characteristics of this period of Venetian dominion were the island's organised administration and the bestowment of religious freedom to its inhabitants. Despite the island's frequently "renewed" population, the Zakynthian element does not fade away. On the contrary, revived through the addition of new cultural elements, it becomes all the more characteristic and strong, succeeding in influencing the island's foreign inhabitants. Once again in the history of the Ionian islands, we come across the incredible ability of local inhabitants to adopt and assimilate the very finest elements of other foreign cultures encountered, and incorporate these into their own tradition without affecting their own local characteristics.

The years go by peacefully and the Zakynthians, now encouraged, start creating small communities beyond the city's walls. In the meantime, Aigialos, as the city was known, is inhabited to capacity and has began to extend beyond castle limits, all the way to the sea. Within a few years the city acquires large squares, well-designed roads and beautiful buildings of such architectural quality as to lend it the name of "The Florence of Greece".

During the governing of Zakynthos - as was the case with all Venetian territories in the Ionian - the Venetian adopted an oligarchic aristocratic regime and the island became a self-administered community with a Council of Aristocrats determining its administration. A Supreme Ruler (so-called Provider) is voted-in with powers extending over all political, judicial and military matters. He, in turn, receives orders and is monitored at times by his supervisor and general ruler of the Ionian islands, who resides in Corfu.

The population is divided- according to the laws that existed more-or-less in all Venetian ruled territories- separated into the three following social classes:
* the Gentry or Nobili, who were registered in the Libro d'Oro and who include people with income from real estate
* the Bourgeoisie or Civili, i.e. the middle class of people who do not enjoy the benefit of political rights, including tradesmen, teachers, priests and all those who are in business for themselves. The bourgeois were half gentry - everyone wanted to be included in this class - and half common people or plebes.
* the Plebes or Popolari, the third social class which includes all those involved in manual labour. This class of people was the most unprivileged, full of duties and no rights. Apart from cultivating the island's soil - land being the island's most significant source of income - the plebes would be recruited by the gentry for defence purposes. The situation at times would become unbearable and exploitation would be severe but, in view of the suffering of those Greeks subjected to Turkish tyranny, the island's inhabitants exercised great patience and waited.

The "Friendly" church of Aghios Georgios

The years of peace are often interrupted by wars and conflicts. In 1499, the conflict between Venice and Turkey breaks out and Zakynthos becomes a supply depot for the Venetian and French fleet. After the end of the war, Venice signs an accord with the Sultan Selim with which, according to its conditions, wheat worth 500 ducats will be transported from Zakynthos to Venice as payment for the taxes paid to the Sultan this far. In the meantime, during the reign of Souleiman, another war between Venice and Turkey breaks out and the island's inhabitants will once again be subjected to looting and devastation, but this time from Barbarosa and the Algerian admiral Uluzeli. During the years that followed, fighting on their own and at times alongside their neighbouring islands, the Zakynthians were able to halt many invasions. A number of Zakynthians with their own ships will sail to help the Greeks in the naval battle of Nafpaktos in 1571, during which the Christian fleet led by the Austrian Don Jouan manages to crush the Turks. All this time, the gentry continue to exploit the lower social classes and mainly the plebes. The local bourgeois and the plebes rise against the gentry in what is the first - during this period - common middle and lower class revolution in Europe: the "rebellion of the Rabble" as it was known (1628 - 1632). The revolt is repressed by the general ruler, Antonio Pisani, delegated by Venice to restore the peace.

In the meantime, life on the island experiences constant turbulence: when there's no war or enemy attack, its inhabitants' lives are threatened by deadly diseases and epidemics.

During the Cretan war (1645 - 1669) the Ionian islands will play a leading role in the battles against the Turks. In the end, however, the Venetian loose the castles on Crete and capitulate with the Turks by surrendering control of Crete on condition to stop taxes for the control of Zakynthos. At this stage, many Cretan families abandon their homeland and flee to Zakynthos. Among these, the ancestors of our national poet, Dionysios Solomos. Cretan civilisation flourishes on the island and adds a new spark to Zakynthos' cultural development.

During the new war between the Venetian and the Turks, Zakynthos will suffer the plague (1688) which will decimate its inhabitants. The Zakynthians will adopt a procession of Aghios Georgios to commemorate their salvation and free travel within the island (30-1-1689).

In 1770, Catherina II, Queen of Russia, incites a national liberation movement in the Peloponnese, the so-called "Orloffian Risings". Despite orders to the contrary from Venice, the Zakynthians participate with an expeditionary force. However, the move fails and Zakynthos is once again obliged to take in refugees from the enslaved parts of Greece. In order to flee the vengeful rage of their conqueror, some 8.000 inhabitants from the Peloponnese come and seek refuge on the island.

The Venetian Democracy, by this stage weakened by successive wars, is in definite decline. The greediness and poor management of many of the gentry provoke the outrage of the common classes, who've had enough of injustice and exploitation. The Zakynthians wait for the opportune moment to fight for their rights and freedom.

The reverberations from the French Revolution (1789) reach all the way to the Ionian islands, where inhabitants now moved and heartened will demand equality, self-determination and justice. This kind of ideology blossoms quickly in a land where human rights have been violated for centuries.

Feeding on a great passion for new ideas, the Zakynthians established cultural societies on their island, the most famous of these included the "Jacobinic Club". Significant authors and poets, as well as popular personalities were members of this club. The Jacovites of Zakynthos demanded that the land be distributed to all civilians and that they be treated equally and granted equal political rights with members of the gentry. The island's landlords fought to retain their rights but were unable to stop the changes that followed. The democratic period of San Marco had finally come to an end.

In July 1797, the flag of the French democrats is raised triumphantly over the castle of Zakynthos. The inhabitants, believing to have turned a new page in the history of their island, burn the "Golden Bible" of the gentry and symbolically plant the "tree of Freedom" in San Marco's square.

The French, led by the Provisional French Governor, Charles De Guy, set up the "presidency of the Town Hall", without the participation of members of the gentry. They abolished the gentry titles and divided the island into counties, the administration of which featured the participation of the bourgeois, farmers and common people. Zakynthos was declared the capital of the "County of the Aegean Sea" and schools for all children were founded.

The economic and social problems, however, were not easy to solve and, furthermore, the French were facing trouble from the gentry who were fuelling anarchy on the island. The blockade by the English makes matters worse and, consequently, the French are ousted after only 15 months.

RUSSIAN & TURKISH OCCUPATION - THE IONIAN STATE

Despite the winds of democracy blowing through Europe, monarchs would not surrender their arms. Turkey, England, Russia, Portugal and Naples succeed in ousting the liberal French from eastern countries. The Russians join forces with the Turks and after the defeat of the French fleet in the naval battle of Abukir, in 1798, will try to take Zakynthos from a now-weakened France.

While the Russian-Turkish fleet besieges the island, a few of the local landlords symbolically surrender the keys of the town to the Russian, thereby forcing the French Guard to surrender in October 1798. The island's gentry celebrate the return of oligarchy, which restores them many of their previously stripped powers. However, they fear that Russian domination will not be long-lived and in order to safeguard their privileges turn towards the oligarchic state of England.

In March 1800, in Constantinople, Russia and Turkey decide to establish the Ionian State, which officially represented the first independent Greek state and lasted seven years. In reality, however, the Ionian State was governed by Russia, who in turn paid a yearly tax to Turkey.

The inhabitants of both Zakynthos and the other Ionian islands, unable to take this sort of exploitation any longer, revolt. The democrat politician, Antonios Martinegos, organises a movement and declares Zakynthos independent from the Ionian State. Hoping to attract the support of a super-power, in February 1801 he raises the English flag over the castle in Zakynthos. However, the Turks negotiate with the English and reinstate Zakynthos in the Ionian State up to 1807, when for about a period of two years the island falls once again in the hands of the French - this time it is soldiers manages to conquer the castle in Zakynthos and declares the town the capital of the Ionian State.

The very first goal the English set was to organise the island's administration and establish a public health system which was absent up to that time. The establishment of the public printing house on the island,

A list with Friendly members

the turn of the imperial French.

ENGLISH RULE - THE FRIENDLY SOCIETY

After the brief interval of French domination on the island, in September 1809 the English fleet with some 3.000 which amongst others also printed the "Journal of the Liberated Islands", was a major cultural event.

The English contributed towards the island's water supply and roads; in fact, a large portion of the island's road network constructed is still used today. Part of the breakwater constructed in that period is currently still in use. The English also undertook the repair-work of a number of old churches and bell-towers in many villages, while at the same time constructed manors outside the town, thereby also influencing the island's architectural character.

In 1814, the large powers of partial and arbitrary administrative policies.

In February 1821, the Zakynthians officially complained to King George the 4th of England, asking him to revise the constitution, but to no avail.

In the meantime the Greeks, inspired by the idea of freedom, establish the

Inside the "Friendly" church of Aghios Georgios

those times decided to establish the independent "United States of the Ionian Islands" which gave the overall administration to the English and the right to appoint their own ruler in Corfu. The new constitution was first enforced by the British ruler, Thomas Maitland, who became famous for his

Friendly Society. In December 1818, the company's headquarters are transferred to Zakynthos. The Friendly members of Zakynthos would be sworn in at the church of Aghios Georgios, situated in the area of Psiloma overlooking the town. The first to be sworn in at Aghios Georgios was Theodoros

44

Kolokotronis, who was followed by a number of famous and brave chieftains from the rest of Greece. With architects such as Pangalos, Papas and Romas, in 1824 the "Commission for the Struggle for Zakynthos" was established, which offered invaluable help during the siege of Mesologhi. Thanks to its activities and diplomatic moves, the Friendly Society was characterised as the "Ministry of Foreign Affairs of Revolutionary Greece".

During the same period, Antonios Martinengos founds a party that acts as the opposition to Maitland's authoritarian regime. The English ruler does not hesitate to sentence him to prison and exile many of his famous followers. Many of his friends struggle to gain him a pardon, which is finally granted by the King of England, and Martinengos is once again able to offer his services to the country.

In the years that follow, thousands of Zakynthians sail across to the Peloponnese and fight alongside other Greeks. Despite the initial disapproval of the English, Zakynthos will eventually develop into a centre of anglophile revolutionaries, aiming at English support for the Greek revolution.

THE END OF ENGLISH RULE - UNION TO GREECE

While the rest of Greece is fighting for its freedom, Zakynthos will make significant steps forward in the field of education. By 1832 the island boasts 37 schools in operation, while in 1836 the first private institution is established, offering tuition in such basic subjects as Greek, Italian and History.

The existence of a free Greek State boosts the efforts of the Ionian islands to gain their independence and be united to the rest of Greece. The free spirit of the Zakynthians can no longer be contained. Long before freedom of press is achieved on the island, the first newspapers are already being printed: the literary paper "Spinthir" (= Spark) is published in 1847 and followed two years later by the political paper "Mellon" (= Future). During the same year, i.e. 1849, the cultural society "O Foskolos" is also established.

The first step towards the independence of the Ionian islands is achieved when censorship is finally lifted and the island's inhabitants are granted voting rights. Three parties are then established in Zakynthos: the Radicals, the Reformists and the Rich.

The Radicals, representing the will of most of the island's inhabitants, aimed at ousting the English and achieving the annexation of the Ionian islands to the Greek State. The Reformists, somewhat more conservative, asked for improvements and changes in order to achieve a better coexistence of Greeks and English in the Ionian islands. Lastly, the Rich represented in a way the voice of the English, provoking the hatred of the other Zakynthians who would call them "Deceitful" and "Behind the times".

After the first free elections which took place on February 28 1850, the ratio of ministers appointed by Zakynthos in the Ionian Parliament were significantly in favour of the Radicals who managed to win 30 seats as opposed to the Reformists with only 4 and the Rich with 6.

In the meantime both Ionian politicians and intellectuals are applying pressure on England to withdraw its protection from the Ionian islands. In December 1851, the member of parliament Ioannis Typaldos-Kapeletos submits a proposal to the Ionian Parliament to hold a vote for the unification of the Ionian islands to Greece. The English retaliate, but the Zakynthians led by the radical Konstantinos Lomvardos are not discouraged. The morale of the locals and their fighting spirit cannot be contained any further, as the political scene in Europe has changed and independence is now only a matter of time.

In December 1858, the special envoy of Queen Victoria of England, W. E. Gladstone, a famous grekophile, is sent to Zakynthos to examine the question of independence, while rumours suggest that England is ready to give the matter some serious consideration.

After the ousting of King Otto from Greece, he is replaced by the Dane, George the 1st,

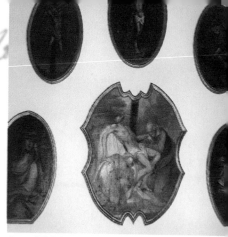

An exhibit in the Museum of Post-Byzantine Art

who is favoured by the English Court, and England accepts to surrender the Ionian islands to the Greek State.

On May 21 1864, the Greek flag is finally raised over the castle in Zakynthos in a triumphant outburst of emotion and enthusiasm by all the island's inhabitants. A couple of months later, the Zakynthians will welcome the new King of Greece on their own territory.

Following centuries of foreign occupation, the Ionian islands are finally able to join their future with that of the rest of Greece and follow a common historical path. The island's previous glory, however, was never lost and remained dispersed and unique in the town of Zakynthos, as a constant reminder of the island's glorious cultural heritage. Unfortunately, the destructive earthquake in 1953 put an end to this vivid image, leaving the town of Zakynthos with no more than the "air" of its once glorious past.

Culture

ARTS & CRAFTS
"Little Paris"

During that period, some twenty five years before the end of the 19th century, the small land of Zakynthos was still in full cultural bloom. Its visitors would call it "Little Paris" and very rightly so. The island was overflowing with wealth, beauty, education, art-lovers and taste.

Under the purest of skies, in untamed natural surroundings, and by the gentle waters of the sea, one would be captivated by glorious manors, palaces and churches that represented exemplary works of art. The island's inhabitants would gather in a cosy theatre and enjoy top quality performances by Italian melodramatic companies, which at times - unbelievable as it may seem - would stage the operas of local composers. The philharmonic band would play twice weekly in one of the two squares in town.

The reading-rooms of the main Clubs and Casinos would offer inhabitants the chance to read from all major European newspapers and leading magazines - French Reviews, English and Italian weekly editions, as well as local publications which were equally important such as "Aganissa", "Korinna", "Zakynthio Anthon" and "Kypseli". There was also a small public library and every proper manor would feature its own personal large collection of books. Strata Marina and Psiloma - the island's famous walk-ways - were honoured on a daily basis. The island would stage grand ecclesiastical feasts and processions, glorious folk fêtes, high calibre aristocratic dances and colourful carnival celebrations. There were captivating firework displays and one would come across luxurious private carriages with great horses and servants dressed in impressive uniforms. Ladies and girls of the aristocracy would stroll along the footpaths in their splendid outfits and fancy hats.

This was the calibre of civilisation that blossomed once upon a time in one of Greece's most distant corners, in the small land of Zakynthos that had only just become part of Greece thanks to the strong and faithful country spirit of its inhabitants who sacrificed some of their most vital interests to this end..." These are the words used by the great Zakynthian literary man, Grigorios Xenopoulos, to describe the island of Zakynthos in his play the "Great Love". Many years have passed since then and Zakynthos has changed along with its customs and people. Or has it?

A great love of arts, music and theatre blossomed throughout the Ionian islands during a period in which the rest of Greece was suffering under Turkish oppression, which reaped the country of any form of freedom or cultural development. And one of the things that remains very much unaffected is the spirit of the island's inhabitants, their great passion for arts and crafts.

POETRY & LITERATURE

Over the centuries, Zakynthos has produced highly significant personalities, whose contributions have shaped the island's cultural image and influenced the life of recent generations in more ways than one.

The blossoming of literature on the island was evident by the 15th century, when many of its writers and poets were acquiring fame for their poetry and prose. Nikolaos Loukanis, a poet and translator of Homer's Iliad, was one of the most famous literary personalities of those times. Other famous literary personalities of that era included Pachomios

An old fountain in town

Rousanos, Dimitrios Zinos, Tzannes Koronaios etc.

Poetry, composition, translation and prose were booming on the island and these works, most of which were printed in Venice, were very well received both by Greek and foreign literary enthusiasts. In the 16th century, the very first Greek Academy is established in Zakynthos, and in 1815 the "Academy of Liberated Meridian Islands" is founded.

The continuous interaction of the island with cultures in Europe and Crete, affect Zakynthian literature, which was influenced by European literature, the Cretan school, folk songs and the work of modern poets. Zakynthian literature loves to praise the importance of religion, country, woman and nature. The peak of the island's cultural development is reached in the 19th century with the birth of Andreas Kalvos and Dionysios Solomos.

Andreas Kalvos (1792 - 1896) was born in Zakynthos, but spent most of his life in Europe. He started his work by writing tragedies in Italian, but his love for his country was what led him to compose the twenty classical "Odes", which were innovative poems, filled with a musical character and inspired by the Greek War of Independence of 1821. The language he uses is a particular form of purist Greek with many elements of demotic. His verse "Freedom requires courage and virtue" will inspire peoples' struggle for freedom for many years to come.

Kalvos' contemporary, Dionysios Solomos was born in Zakynthos in 1798 and died in Corfu in 1857. He studied and lived many years in Italy, dividing his time in Greece between his two favorite islands, Zakynthos and Corfu. His work combines romantic and classic themes with the passion for "freedom and speech", in the critical spirit that created the prose the "Woman of Zakynthos", which has been classified as one of the finest examples of modern Greek literature.

In 1864, verses from his poem entitled the "Hymn to Liberty", set to music by Nikolaos Mantzaros, the famous musician from Corfu, become our country's National Anthem. Another highlight of his work is the poem entitled "The Free Besieged", written during the poet's most mature period and dedicated to the fighters in Mesologhi.

A short time after his death, the school of poets called the "Ionian School" was founded, its main members being Iakovos Polylas, Ioulios Typaldos, Georgios Tertsetis, and the brothers Andreas and Stefanos Martzokis.

Another important personality of Zakynthos' tradition is Elizabeth Moustan-Martinengou (1801 - 1832), who was one of the very first Greek women authors to win a place in our country's literary history thanks to her highly important "Autobiography".

The Italian-speaking poet, Nikolaos Oungo Foskolos, was born and educated in Zakynthos. His poem entitled "The Tombs" established him as Italy's National poet. The historian and lexicographer Leonidas Ch. Zois (1865 - 1956) contributed a great deal to the work of his predecessors, historians and explorers. His work is still considered an invaluable source of the island's history and folklore.

Last but by no means least, Grigorios Xenopoulos (1867 - 1951) dominated the scene with his immense contribution, as an author and theatrical playwright, to the more recent history of the island. As a prose and theatrical playwright, a great critic and reporter, in 1931 he was nominated as a member of the Academy. The greatest part of his work is inspired by the life and

The past of Solomou square

society of Zakynthos, the island that he loved the most. He was also noted for his significant contribution to the establishment of demotic Greek in novels and theatrical plays. In fact, his plays are still staged in theatres around the country and succeed in attracting considerable public interest.

MUSIC

Music and song have always played an important role in life on Zakynthos. From antiquity, the island's inhabitants worshipped Apollo, the mythological god of music. All the way back then, Zakynthians mad expressed their love of music by minting a coin whose one side depicted their local musician Pythagoras and on the other the lyre.

One only need to walk through the streets of Zakynthos and listen to people's conversations and teasing to realise how this bond between music and speech was created and why serenading was born here. Western musical influences were combined with Ionian custom to create a result which has become famous all over the country, and often accompanied by mandolins and string orchestras. The taverns in Bochali still echo the verse "my light, I wished to be the dreams in your sleep".

Apart from serenading, Zakynthos was also the birthplace of "arekia", a folk song which is sung by a quartet of four different voices. This traditional type of song, which was inspired locally, features the peculiarity of the third voice, or "terza". Another passion on the island, was its inhabitants love of opera and operetta, which also brought the aristocracy closer to the people. Lastly, Zakynthos was also the place where melodrama blossomed: in fact, the theatre in

town was the venue for the very first performance of an operetta in Greece.

The first Music School in Zakynthos was established in 1815 by the Italian professor Marco Batajia. The Philharmonic of Zakynthos, established in 1816, is considered to be the oldest in Greece. During the years that followed, a number of choruses and philharmonics were established in town and in the villages around the island, many of which are still performing today. Zakynthos' philharmonic excelled in a number of contests and made an appearance in the 1869 Olympic Games. Apart from the official venues, Zakynthians were often given the opportunity to listen to the Philharmonic in out-door performances, which were held in squares and often called "plateies" (= squares).

To this day, the Philharmonic still represents an integral part of all processions and festivities, with its musicians lending a different note to a number of fêtes and, as in the past, often performing in out-door concerts.

The island's significant musical tradition has created a large number of great musicians, whose fame has stretched throughout Greece. Among these, Pavlos Karrer who is considered to be the forerunner of Modern Greek Music, Frangiskos Domeneginis, Antonis Kapnisis and many more.

THEATRE

Theatre blossomed in Zakynthos during Venetian rule, initially influenced by the Italian Folk Theatre of the Middle Ages and the Renaissance. The "Persians" by Aeschylus, in Italian, along with comedies, ancient Greek and Italian plays are staged in the so-called "literary" halls of those times. During

54

The outfit of an old noblewoman

ΠΟΛΙΣ ΖΑΚΥΝΘΟΥ
ΑΡΧΟΝΤΙΣΣΑΣ

the final years of Venetian rule, a small theatre was built in Zakynthos and would regularly attract both cultured aristocrats and common folk, who were driven to these performances by their innate passion for theatre.

The Zakynthian passion for sarcasm, which most probably helped alleviate the oppression of the gentry, led to the creation of a particular type of theatre, known as the Discourses/Dialogues. The development of theatrical speech on the island was also greatly influenced by the arrival of refugees from Crete, who settled in the Ionian islands after the destruction of Chandakas, currently the city of Herakleion. Both the structure and the improvising manner in which these Discourses/Dialogues were played, suggest that they originated from the union between the Venetian Commedia dell'Arte and the Cretan theatrical scene.

Marietta Giannopoulou-Minotou describes the Discourses/Dialogues in the following manner: "In Zakynthos what we call Discourses/Dialogues are theatrical plays which common people hold in the out-doors during carnival. The satires were written by young noblemen and would portray aristocratic balls, famous fêtes, the sale of brides and grooms and many more. The custom is definitely Venetian. The famous carnival in Venice is reflected through present-day carnival celebrations in Zakynthos.

The Discourses/Dialogues begin on "Tsouchnopempti", Carnival Thursday and continue to Quinquagesima, shrove Sunday. On these days, if the skies were clear and the sun shone through, the Discourses/Dialogues would begin from about two in the afternoon in front of the wealthiest homes, in the most central parts of town and in village squares.

There are always a couple of stage-directors and one or two more eccentrically disguised individuals that are responsible for maintaining peace in the audience...

Until a few years ago, inhabitants would stage famous plays like Erotokritos, Erofili, and The Sacrifice of Abraham always customised according to the island's tradition and changed to suit peoples' preferences.

Any boring acts are altogether excluded from the performance. We are not certain if the Discourses/Dialogues began in Zakynthos with the arrival of Cretan refugees or if, before the fall of Crete, Cretan Theatre had already reached these shores. However, there were definitely Discourses/Dialogues during Venetian rule...

Discourses/Dialogues are staged by men alone, the most handsome of which play the role of women, disguised in flashy women's clothing and wearing white false pearls and face-masks, not those made of cloth, but rather those that actually portray a female face...

As the changing of scenes is not easy, the actors stand at right angles to eachother. The main characters are at the top, with the others opposite on either side. When the scene changes, the actors who up to that moment would be amongst the spectators, would suddenly appear or disappear accordingly..."

Starting from the Discourses/Dialogues, Zakynthos developed a significant theatrical tradition: numerous theatres were built and ancient dramas were staged, as well as plays from the Cretan theatrical scene and those written by modern Zakynthian playwrights.

A window-sill in full bloom

The gold-embellished icon-screen of in Aghia Mavra

PAINTING

Zakynthos has a great deal to be proud of in the field of Fine Arts. Many famous hagiographers from all over the country lived and created on Zakynthos, the works and icons of which adorn many of the island's churches to our days.

The existing styles adopted were influenced significantly by the arrival of Cretan artists, who settled in Zakynthos after the destruction of Chandakas, in the mid 17th century. The most important of these artists include Michail Damaskinos, Dimitrios and Georgios Moschos, Manolis and Konstantinos Tzannes, and Stefanos Tzangarolas. The works of these artists are currently preserved in a number of churches around the island and in the Post-Byzantine Art Museum in town.

Most of the icons adorning the island's churches belong to the Creto-Zakynthian School of Art. The arrival of the Cretan on Zakynthos influences almost every artistic field, yielding the basis for the creation of an entirely new school of thought and style, which incorporates elements from both islands. The same degree of influence is also evidenced in ecclesiastical music and harmonic music for four voices.

The main characteristic of Zakynthian painting is the naturalistic style, influenced by Italian renaissance, and which in combination to Byzantine technique, gave birth to the Ionian School of Art. During the 17th and 18th century, the Ionian School of Art focused mainly on hagiographies and religious subjects in general.

However, towards the end of the 18th century and the start of the 19th, its creations begin to address cosmopolitan subjects, more often than not depicting scenes from everyday life. Among the most important representatives of the Ionian School of Art one recalls Panagiotis Doxaras, Nikolaos

Koutouzis, Nikolaos Kantounis etc. Over the next years, younger painters keep the tradition alive by combining it with their own styles. The works of Dionysios Tsokos, Al. and G. Gryparis, and Dimitrios Pelekasis manage to bring painting closer to the people, not merely as a means of depicting the divine but as a work of art that actually targets the senses.

SILVER & WOODCARVING

The churches in Zakynthos bear witness to the blossoming of the art of carving, which was introduced no the island around the 17th century. Most of its churches are adorned with highly impressive icon-screens carved in stone or wood. In fact, the island's bell-towers, like for example that of Aghios Nikolaos in Koiliomeno, represent unique artistic and structural achievements. To this day, many inhabitants in mountain villages across Zakynthos are still wood and stone carvers.

Among its most famous wood carvers, one recalls Anastasios Vlachos and the Andraviotis brothers who, along with Timotheos Kefalonitis, were the artists behind the creation of the icon-screen in Aghios Dionysios.

Zakynthian artists are also famous for their great craftsmanship and talent in silver carving. Among the most famous of these one recalls Diamantis and Georgios Balafas who created the silver reliquary that holds the relics of Aghios Dionysios.

Apart from the writer Grigorios Xenopoulos, the same family was famous once again for the significant mosaics created by his brother Stefanos. Many of his works currently adorn churches in Zakynthos and in other parts of Greece.

ARCHITECTURE

The close ties that the Ionian islands had with the west were responsible for the particular architectural character witnessed in their towns. Another important influencing factor was the climate on these islands, which is generally warm and mild all year long. The fine weather and sunshine of the Ionian climate would drive people outdoors. Hence their homes featured large balconies, semi-exposed areas and porches. Their buildings also featured galleries, which were vital in Ionian towns, offering inhabitants easy refuge in the case of common and sudden downpours. So for all those who had left home without an umbrella there was always a chance to avoid getting soaked, by walking under the arched protection of these galleries.

A classic example of the architecture adopted during the 19th century was the clubhouse "o Zakynthos", situated in Aghios Marcos' square, and which was destroyed during the 1953 earthquakes, along with most of the island's old buildings. The town's Municipal Theatre was another fine architectural example of those times, designed by the famous German architect Ernest Tschiller, and which also housed the club "Lomvardos".

In old Zakynthos, the aristocratic houses were domineering, the oldest of which had been built under the influence of the Renaissance, at first, and neo-classical tendencies later on. The island's rocky soil was ideal for the artistic creativity of local designers. Manors in town were usually three storey buildings, some of which were built in the centre and others overlooking the sea or near the bays in the direction of Kryoneri. Hosts would welcome their visitors in their entrances or "basia", usually ornate with pots and colourful flowers.

During times of Venetian rule, these manors would actually resemble

Flowers on the island

palaces, each one having its own stable, a chapel, the priest's cell and caretaker's quarters. In many cases, these aristocratic residences comprised a number of auxiliary buildings, creating a separate complex or block, which would be named after the landlord.

In Ammos there used to be a long string of almost identical homes, with columns like those standing on Rouga Square. These were the homes of the bourgeois or the common people and included a small Casino, as the locals used to call their clubs.

Of all the exotic aristocratic villas on the island, the only surviving one is the Saracena, a characteristic example of the architecture of the times, which belongs to the Lountzis family and is situated near the village of Pantokratoras.

The homes of the bourgeois and the plebes were naturally less impressive, but nonetheless influenced by the architectural tendencies of upper-class buildings. Both in town and in the countryside, one comes across homes painted in the Ionian colours, ochre (a yellowish-orange-red tint), terracotta and purple.

The earthquake was disastrous for the whole island and more importantly for the town itself, levelling almost every one of its buildings. The squares, however, were redecorated and surrounded by beautiful buildings, that take one back to good-old Zakynthos, and Strata Marina was restored and once again features horse-and-carriage rides. The island's authentic image is nowadays only visible on old and weathered pictures. The new Zakynthos stands proud with its bell towers and flower-clad balconies, exuding the air of its magical and glorious past.

Folklore

RELIGION - PROCESSIONS

Zakynthos is an island with a very strong sense of religion. In fact most of its Christian celebrations have been preserved intact through time. The processions still manage to impress both locals and foreigners with the ceremonial and official manner, and the most important of these still attract people from all over the country year after year.

Prior to the 1953 earthquakes, visitors to the island would encounter churches and monasteries everywhere in town and in each and every village. Until that time, the island still retained about 300 of the 600 orthodox churches that existed during Venetian rule.

The holy relics of Aghios Dionysios still dominate the town and indeed the entire island. Aghios Dionysios was the island's patron Saint and two

Worshippers' hope for salvation

The temple of Aghios Dionysios, the island's patron saint

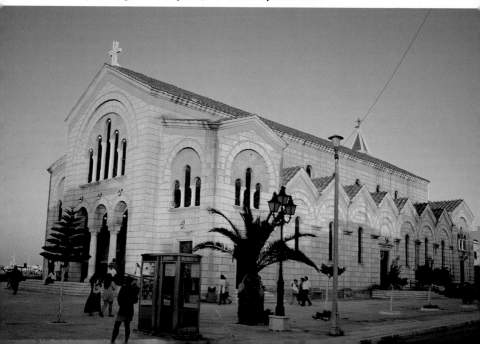

yearly celebrations are held in his name. His Assumption on December 17th and the transportation of his remains from Strofades to Zakynthos on August 24th. This apart, there are many more feasts that are celebrated in a similar glorious manner on the island. The feast of the Holy Mary, on August 15th, and which is considered by the church as the summertime Easter, is celebrated with a series of processions that involve the entire island and attract a large number of visitors.

Impressive celebrations are also held on the feast of Aghios Dionysios, Aghios Nikolaos, Aghia Varvara and during Christmas, the latter also featuring the customary Christmas bun. Easter on Zakynthos is another major event, which is also characterised by traditional celebrations during the Easter Week. The procession to Aghios Dionysios, which is probably the most important occasion for the faithful in Zakynthos and in many other parts of Greece, is celebrated in a grand manner every year without fail. In 1953, just eleven days after the devastating earthquake that levelled the town, the procession was held in the usual manner, following the usual route, which involved the use of earth-moving equipment to clear away the rubble. The Zakynthians had come out into the streets to mourn the suffering of their Saint, Aghios Dionysios, along with their own as they stood in front of their destroyed and burnt homes. The processions always feature members of local authorities, the clergy, the island's inhabitants and thousands of worshippers who flock Zakynthos to witness the Holy Relics, believed to have miraculous powers. Dozens of worshippers lie on the street in front of the procession, in hope of a cure should the relics pass over them.

This evening procession is truly

Scenes from the Saint's procession

65

The start of a procession

spectacular! Colourful lanterns held by worshippers lend their light to the procession, while priests chant dressed in their very best cassocks, the Saint's bell-tower dominates above the town all lit up, and the locals create an impressive display of fireworks to honour their Saint. The feast of Aghia Mavra is almost equally important as the procession of her icon around Machairados, where the Saint's church is situated, attracts thousands of worshippers every year.

EASTER

The Passion Week or Easter Week leading to Easter Sunday is celebrated in Zakynthos with great devotion and emotion. Easter celebrations and the days of the Easter Week are characterised by customs and traditions that have always played a major role in life on the island. So from Palm Sunday every bell house hangs a branch of palm, while from Mourn-day Thursday

The worship of Aghios Dionysios

the island's church bells are "widowed" and do not sound until the morning of Easter Saturday. Throughout the Easter Week, priests wear black vestments and during the processions people hang black banners, called "pefkia", from their balconies. The Easter Sepulchre Procession and Madre Dolorosa is held on Good Friday, at noon. The procession sets off from the chapel of Aghios Nikolaos in Molos, crosses through town and ends in Solomos square. At that point, the bishop takes the stand and blesses the four points of the horizon. The ceremony, called the "Blessing of the Universe", is accompanied by the sounds of a piece of music chosen especially for the occasion. Rumour has it that the piece played by the band was composed centuries ago by a local musician.

One of the most emotional moments during the Easter Week is the Easter Sepulchre Procession which travels through town to the sound of the Philharmonic band playing funeral hymns. The procession starts at the Cathedral of Aghios Nikolaos ton Xenon. On Good Friday, in remembrance of the Holy Passion, people drink vinegar and women throw terracotta jugs from their windows. This unique Easter Sepulchre Procession is actually not carried out on Good Friday in the afternoon, but rather in the early morning hours of Easter Saturday. At dawn the procession returns to church whereby church bells all over town ring joyously to announce the Holy Saturday Morning Service, "Gloria of the Crucifix" as the Zakynthians call it. Priests change their black vestments for red joyous ones and the band fills the night with joyful triumphal hymns.

The Easter Night Service, as in the rest of Greece, is celebrated at midnight on Good Saturday, on San Marco square. The anchored ships blow their whistles to the sound of "Christos Anesti" (= Jesus has risen), which is drowned in the bursts of fireworks and church-bells ringing. Easter Sunday is forever imprinted in

Zakynthian countryside

one's memory for the smell of burning lamb on the spit, which rises from literally every home and street-corner, and for the fragrance of local wine. On Easter Monday, processions carrying icons portraying scenes from the Resurrection are moved through every village, to the sound of Gloria, Hosanna in excelsis.

FETES

In the old days, fêtes used to represent the most popular feasts both in Zakynthos and in most other parts of Greece. The church of the village that was about to hold a fête would be up-and-about days before the feast, in order to manage all the necessary preparations. Worshippers and peddlers would arrive from every village on Zakynthos, while women would prepare their most beautiful outfits for the occasion. To our days, major fêtes give both locals and those living abroad the chance to meet again and visit their homeland.

The most famous of the island's fêtes are those that follow the feasts of Aghios Dionysios, Aghios Timotheos and Aghia Mavra. On most occasions, the Municipal Philharmonic accompanies both the mass and the procession of the icon being

Delicacies and fêtes

celebrated.

Another important feast on the island is that of the Saints Konstantinos and Eleni, which for the Ionian islands represents a double celebration as it coincides with the anniversary of their union to Greece. From the very old days, the island's Cathedral has always held a service (Te Deum) on the morning of the 21st of May to commemorate the island's Union to Greece. And in the afternoon, the Zakynthians would be in the streets once again visiting all the island's "Ntantos", as they like to refer to those called Konstantinos. In the evening, the entire island as well as those neighbouring it, would watch the display of fireworks originating from the town square.

Another significant fête in Zakynthos is the feast of the Ascension of Christ, during which the island's landlords would traditionally participate with dancing and fun until the early morning hours. On Rouga square - presently A. Roma street - it was customary to roast lamb and all the island's gentry and bourgeois were supposed to buy meat off the street in order to support the lower classes, the Popolari. Another known custom during fêtes had worshipers selling livestock, honey and cheese in support of the celebrating church.

The feast of Aghios Lazaros is also among the largest fêtes and is held on Easter Sunday and on Trinity Sunday, the latter lasting three days. Worshipers eat pasteli - honey and sesame seed bar - and frytoura - fried dessert made of semolina and sugar - in makeshift kiosks and dance and sing to music. Musicians prepare their marquees the day before and let their music create the appropriate atmosphere.

On Easter Sunday in the evening, the church of Aghios Lazaros would stage its own feast. The procession would be followed by a fête with songs and

Selling crusifixes and icons

dancing, lamb on the spit and fireworks.

The feast of Zoodochou Pigi (= the source of life) (Chryssopigi) is held on Easter Week Friday, in Bochali. A procession of the Byzantine icon of the Madonna Chryssopigi is carried out in the streets of the suburb: a fête that follows with music, food and wine, lasts until the early morning hours.

CUSTOMS & LOCAL WAYS

In one of his features in the newspaper "Eleftheria" (= freedom), Dionysis Romas had given his personal theory, which is quite right, about the Zakynthian anteti: "The anteti is a Zakynthian custom and involves the yearly repetition of a specific gesture, in the scope of establishing a personal tradition." He goes on to say that the anteti can even involve "participating in a certain ceremony, a religious mass, or any other event that occurs on a yearly

basis" and which the faithful individual "must not miss even if this means breaking a trip and returning for this reason alone!"

Not just one anteti, but more like a whole group of customs and local ways which are meticulously respected on the island and God help the one that dares to ignore these. Even the ceremonial Easter on Zakynthos includes a series of small and large such customs, which have been carefully respected by priests through the years and never changed or replaced despite opposing church rules.

The anteti is faithfully performed for reasons of good luck, as those who undertake these - called antetadoros - believe that any omission might cast a bad spell. It is quite amazing to think that the Zakynthians observed each and every anteti even amongst the rubble left behind by the earthquake in 1953, when the entire town had been levelled.

Giannis Chrysikopoulos has recorded a number of common anteti's, some of are quite original. According to him, Zakynthians are supposed to eat pork done in the oven on the seventieth day before fasten (septuagesima), on Pancake Day they are supposed to eat fricasseed lamb with rice, and during Carnival almond cake - known as mantolato - and rice pudding. On Palm Sunday it is customary to have cod with garlic sauce, on Good Friday lettuce leaves in vinegar on an un-set table, after the Resurrection beef in egg and lemon soup, on All Saints Day meatballs, on August 15th chicken in the oven, on the summer feast of Aghios Dionysios cod with garlic sauce, on September 14th octopus in tomato sauce with crushed grain, and on Christmas Day turkey in egg and lemon sauce. In Zakynthos they do not cut a New Year Cake, but on Christmas Eve they eat broccoli and cut the customary bread roll, or "kouloura", which the whole family holds over a fire, on which they pour oil and wine.

Apart from the general customs or anteti's described above, the island is also known to have family anteti's and anteti's between friends, both of which are meticulously observed. However, in the evening of Good Friday it is also customary to play jokes - called "mancia" - on friends and relatives.

CARNIVAL

The truly beautiful island of Zakynthos has a great deal to offer every visitor throughout the entire year. As is the case in all the Ionian islands, Venetian domain has left its trademark in the Carnival celebrations, which are staged yearly and involve a great deal of fun, masquerades, dancing and singing in the streets.

Up to the start of our century, the carnival season would begin at the "kavarkines" (folk centres) which would attract youngsters and "maskares" (women disguised with masks), who would live it up all night long. The women of both the aristocracy and the lower classes would wear "mouzeta" or "moretes" (masks), which they would buy from street vendors.

On shrove Sunday in the afternoon, the two main squares in town would witness the largest popular gathering ever. Onions, lettuce and other Lenten foods would be hung from the balcony of the bell-tower of the church of All Saints (Aghioi Pantes) and the large bell would ring to announce the beginning of Lent. The same afternoon would feature the "Povero Karnavali" (= the Poor Carnival), the funeral of the mask. Zakynthians would place a carnival face-mask on a stretcher, which would play the part of a death-bed, and would parade around town as if in a funeral procession. The "funeral" was attended by all the town's inhabitants who would mourn the "death" of their carnival.

Nowadays a few significant island authorities manage to keep these carnival festivities very much alive thanks to the help and undying spirit of the island's inhabitants. The Zakynthian carnival with its joyful and festive atmosphere lasts an entire fortnight. On the second Sunday of carnival, the island holds the "Piccolo Karnavali" (= the Small Carnival) which features the participation of all the island's children, who live it up and dance to music. The large carnival is held on the last Sunday of the fortnight and features the participation of all Zakynthians in colourful processions, who sing and dance in the streets around town. In the evening of the last Sunday, the island stages the Povero Karnavali, which features the burning of the mask to symbolise the end of the Carnival celebrations.

Traditional female outfit

ΧΩΡΙΟΥ
ΜΑΧΑΙΡΑΔΟΥ

WEDDING

People always grasped at the chance to have a good time, even during hardships, in an effort to forget their worries and would wholeheartedly participate in the joyful moments of their fellow islanders. Apart from Zakynthos' fêtes and feasts, weddings were amongst the social events that would affect entire villages and represented an opportunity for days of great fun and entertainment.

In the old days weddings would represent an arranged affair and would rarely involve love. When a wedding was arranged, the two families would at first hold the traditional "skartsofolia", i.e. the marriage contracts would be drawn. The groom and his father, along with the "novaro", the notary, would go to the bride's home and would agree on the dowry to be given to the bride. In this way the bride would receive part of the groom's family wealth and would surrender any further future claims on that. This is not such an old custom and nowadays one still encounters a number of couples who were wed by an arranged marriage and following such an agreement.

Apart from the ceremony in church, a wedding involved a series of traditions and customs which both families would honour before the actual event took place.

Tradition had it that weddings were held only on a Sunday. So, on the Wednesday before the wedding, the bride would hang and display her dowry in her courtyard, for all the village to admire. On Thursday, the bride's home would be full of fellow villagers who would come to congratulate her parents. On Friday, the groom and his father would come to the bride's home and would load her dowry into large trunks, which they would then transport to the couple's new home.

The day before the wedding, i.e. on Saturday, they would make the bridal bed and let little boys sit on it, in the hope of ensuring that the new couple's children would be male, and would throw money on the bed, in order to ensure the couple's future prosperity. The wedding ceremony was usually held in the bride's family home. Her father would unlock every drawer and would place a knife at the house's threshold. Once the couple came before the priest, no one was allowed to enter or leave the house until the ceremony was over.

On the wedding night, once the couple retired after the celebrations, the bride's mother-in-law would inspect the bed's bottom-sheet to ascertain that the bride was indeed a virgin. If it were blood-stained, she would hang it on a stick and display it to all those invited to the wedding, who would start firing their rifles in the air in a sign of approval. However, if the bride were not a virgin, the groom would send the bride back to her father, seated backwards on a donkey!

FOLK DANCES & COSTUMES

Zakynthos boasts a number of highly impressive folk dances. The locals would dance these in every feast and fête, which they would attend dressed and decorated according to their social class.

The Zakynthian syrto (= round), danced throughout the island, features in many areas with small variations and under different names. Volimes and its neighbouring areas dance the Volimian or "Volimiotikos", the "Galariotikos", "Leventiniko" and many others. The "Giargitos" is amongst the most famous of these folk dances and originates from the Cretan dance called "Gerano". This particular dance re-enacts the triumphant dance of Theseus after he slaughtered the Minotaur, and was

XΩPIOY
KATAΣTAPIõ

Women's clothing from Katastari

fêtes, and during normal day-to-day life. The pieces comprising their attire, from their dress to their hats - known as "fournimenta" - were always representative of their social class and age.

During the Middle Ages, women's clothing were more like a dress trimmed in gold and tied around the waist with a piece of thick black braid. A few centuries later, during the 19th century, the island's countesses paid particular attention to their attire and dressed in smart, loose fitting garments. In summer they would add veils and gauzes across their breasts and in winter they would wear long felt dresses.

The elderly women of the aristocracy, who in daily life would dress in style but conservatively, during times of feast would wear velvet gowns. Widows were dressed in black and would wear a white scarf around their heads, which they tied under their jaw. Over this, they would wear another black garment which they would attach to the top of their heads and would lethang freely in the wind.

Men, however, were also known to pay particular attention to their attire, sometimes more so than women. The aristocrats and bourgeoisie in particular would display special finesse in this respect.

On their outings, counts would usually wear luxurious velvet clothing, copying Venetian gentry. Most of them would wear a wig and a triple-creased hat made of black silk and would carefully trim their moustache and beard. In summer they would circulate in light-coloured linen suits, dark shirts, white tie and a hard straw-hat or panama.

The Popolari or plebes would wear a small black hard hat which they would remove in a sign of respect, when talking to their masters. Villagers would tie a wide red-coloured belt around their waist, which would carry

mostly danced in the village of Vougiato. Another dance called the "δmoiri" (= ill-fated) is encountered in Ag. Leontas and describes the misfortunes of a young woman who had an unfortunate wedding. In the area of Kerio, people would dance a folk dance called "Kynigos" (= hunter) and sing the song of the "Kalogrias kai tou Kynigou" (= the Nun and the Hunter). Unfortunately many other traditional dances have long been forgotten and can only be vaguely recalled by a few of the older generations.

Probably influenced by the smart appearance of Venetian women, but also thanks to their innate good taste, Zakynthian women have always taken great care of their appearance, both on special occasions like feasts and their gun.

When village-girls went outdoors they would wear a petticoat or "motolo" with a frill or "kafoumo" and a hand-woven veil or "valesi" with braids. Over this, they would wear a tight jerkin made of black velvet with a crocheted edge. For their housework, they would wear an apron or "kotolo". Examples of traditional Zakynthian dresses are displayed in glass show-cases at the Library in town (see Town).

CURRENT CULTURAL EVENTS

The island of Zakynthos stages a number of events on a yearly basis, most of which are of a cultural context. The island's eventful history, featuring interchanging European conquerors, played an important role in shaping the cultural identity of both Zakynthos and the rest of the Ionian islands in general.

Theatre became particularly popular on the island, especially after the arrival of Cretan refugees following the destruction of Handakas (presently Herakleion). Along with the inhabitants from Crete, Zakynthos was influenced by Cretan civilisation and its people's inclination to music and metrical speech. One of the characteristics resulting from the blend of these two civilisations were the Discourses/Dialogues and Folk Theatre, although researchers have not concluded yet as to whether the Discourses/Dialogues were practised prior to Cretan arrival (see Theatre on page 58).

Around 1962, Zakynthos saw the Interaction of Medieval and Folk Theatre, which due to the adverse political circumstances of that time and despite great efforts was unfortunately discontinued and never acquired the fame it deserved. Thankfully, however, there are still some people who keep the island's tradition deep within themselves, in an effort to revive, albeit in a somewhat different form, a cultural event of international proportions on an island that has produced so many significant intellectuals and personalities.

Presently and mainly during the Carnival season, the villages across the island witness the re-enactment of Discourses/Dialogues, performed solely by men, according to custom. Then again, in town and mainly during the month of August, a number of outdoor performances are held with the participation of the Municipality, the County Council that deals in island cultural events, and a number of the island's cultural societies.

Apart from theatrical plays, the island stages a number of events throughout the year and mainly during summer, during which time visitors will have the chance to see interesting painting exhibitions, as well as photography and many more.

Every August, the Municipal Cultural Department organises the "Zakynthia", a string of cultural events lasting about 10 days. Those who happen to be on the island during that period will have the opportunity to enjoy a number of impressive musical shows, artistic events, concerts by local choruses in the squares around town, and listen to authentic "arekia's" and serenades. Amongst the most captivating such events, one should not miss the so-called "varkarola", which features impressively lit boats with local artists, who fill the evening with the sweet melody of their serenades.

The island manages to attract a great number of visitors every year, who arrive to watch its exciting sporting activities. Every August is the month of the famous International Sailing Week, which starts in Piraeus and, after travelling to all the Ionian islands, ends in Zakynthos.

The town

ZAKYNTHOS TOWN

As the ship approaches the town and main port, visitors are captivated by the tall and ornate bell-towers that decorate Zakynthos town, or Chora as the locals like to call it. The town stretches some 2.5 kilometres, between the hillsides of the Castle and Exintavelonis. The width of the town, which is mostly bound by the island's mountainous landscape, in many places narrows down to a mere 100 metres, while alongside the river of Aghios Charalambous stretches to some 850 metres.

YESTERYEAR...

The massive earthquake in 1953 that levelled the old town, leaving but a few buildings standing,

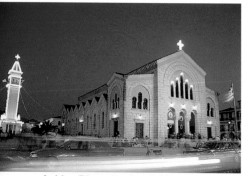

Aghios Dionysios by night
A bird's eye view of Zakynthos

A photo of old Zakynthos

brought a radical change to the island's five-century-strong architecture. However, both the islanders' will to retain the original building plan and the particular layout of the town, "squashed" between the two hills, did not leave room for improvisations. Present-day Zakynthos lies on the original plan of the old town and uses the same road network.

However, the earthquakes that shook the island during the course of its recent past played a major role in determining the layout of the town as it stands today. One need only consider that between 1864 and 1886, Zakynthos was struck by 640 earthquakes!

From about the 16th century onwards, the rubble left behind by each earthquake would be dumped in the sea, reclaiming portions of the island's off-shore formation. This created land for homes built in place of those destroyed as well as giving the opportunity for the establishment of the thousands of refugees that would flee to Zakynthos from other parts of Greece, in an attempt to escape Turkish oppression.

Rouga square, which is currently called Alexandrou Roma street, Lomvardou street - the old Strata Marina - the quarter of Giofyri, are

Past memories

Past memories

still the landmarks that determine the town's character. The Trees of Ammos, Solomou square, St. Marco's square, and the clearance of Faneromeni, have the same shape and function as they did before the earthquakes.

The famous narrow streets or "kantounia" might not exist any more and the earthquake might

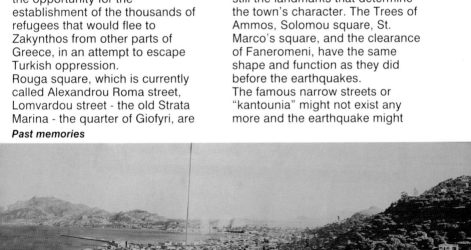

Bell-towers

have destroyed an architectural heritage many centuries long, but Zakynthos still breathes the air of nobility and aristocracy of its glorious past.

TODAY...

Solomou square, situated at the edge of the port's main quay, is the largest such square on the island, similar in size to squares in some major Italian cities. The square sits on reclaimed land, which was land-filled to accommodate the town's expansion. Tiled and adorned with large flower-beds, the square is the centre of life every evening. A meeting place for the young and old, who occupy the tables in the square or buy almond cakes and sesame-bars from the street vendors, Solomou square is still the heart of Zakynthos town.

The buildings around the square generally house local authorities and museums, mostly preserving the area's pre-earthquake character. Single and double-storey aristocratic buildings fringe the square and lend it the image of an old countess. The statue of Dionysios Solomos, in its centre, stands tall and observes the flow of life in what was his favourite town. At the far end, a building constructed after the earthquake, in a neo-classical style with large arches along its facade, houses the Municipal Library, the Cultural Centre and the "Foskolos" movie-theatre.

Aghios Nikolaos of Molos

The first library in Zakynthos, established in 1628, was situated within the original town limits, inside the fortress. The official library was established in 1803, during the period of the state. In 1935 it was united to the Foskolian Library, which was founded in 1888. The massive earthquake that struck the island in 1953 and the fire that followed, turned 33.000 volumes into ashes, amongst which hand-written texts by Kolokotronis and Lord Byron, representing invaluable pieces of Zakynthian history.

Panoramic view of town

One year after its destruction, the library was temporarily housed in the school of Ammos, which had survived, and in 1959 it was finally transferred to its present seat on Solomou square. The new library was created from scratch thanks to offers of books and donations from private individuals, with first and foremost the historian-researcher of Zakynthos, Leonidas Zois. The library currently boasts more than 60.000 volumes, including a number of very rare documents on the island's historical and folkloric heritage, and is being constantly expanded.

Ascending the indoor staircase leading to the main library hall, we have the chance to see a series of rare photos of the old lost town, the lavishly decorated interiors of its old manors, and the interior of temples carved in wood and silver which have all unfortunately perished in the earthquakes. On the first floor of the building, displayed inside glass show-cases, we can admire miniatures in local and traditional Zakynthian outfits.

The ground floor houses the Museum of Occupation and Greek Resistance featuring exhibits from the recent period of Italian and German occupation, as well as from older periods of occupation in the

Solomou square

island's eventful past.

The exhibits in the show-cases in the Museum of Occupation and Greek Resistance present a step-by-step flashback into the history of the Ionian islands, through highly interesting finds, and pieces of the area's old and recent past. Amongst some of the finds that date back several centuries, we distinguish the rare document dating back to the 17th century which bears the signature of the island's patron saint, Aghios Dionysios Sigouros. Also impressive is the baggage inspection tag given to Theodoros Kolokotronis and a copy of the Nafplion Court Decision to sentence both Th. Kolokotronis and D. Plapoutas to death.

On the southern end of Solomou square, the Museum of Post-

Byzantine Art features very interesting works of both Ionian and Cretan artists. The museum is open daily, from Monday, between 8am and 2.30pm.

On the right-hand-side hall on the ground floor, we can admire two carved masterpieces of post-Byzantine icon-screens, belonging to the temples of Ag. Dimitrios of Kollas (1690) and the Pantocrator (1621). The icon-screens were rescued from the destroyed temples, after the devastating

Amongst the main exhibits in the halls on the first floor, one finds carefully preserved and reconstructed frescos from the walls of the church of Ag. Andreas in Volimes. In the halls on the ground floor, we will admire the works of art of Cretan and Ionian artists and painters of the 16th and 17th century, portraying mainly Byzantine thought with certain elements of Italian Renaissance and the Flemish school of art. An impressive scaled model of the town of Zakynthos, as

Aghios Markos' paved square

earthquake, thanks to the invaluable contribution of a number of people, both locals and foreigners, who helped preserve the island's historical heritage. The same hall also exhibits interesting items used in such temples and carved out of wood.

it was before the earthquake, constructed by G. Manesis, is on display in the left-hand-side hall on the ground floor.

Resuming the "exploration" of the town's main square, we come across the church of Ag. Nikolaos of Molos, founded in 1561 by the sailors' guild. At first the church was built on an island located just a few metres off shore, but after successive landfills in the harbour, it eventually became part of the island's mainland. The church of Ag. Nikolaos of Molos is the only Venetian building to have survived the devastating earthquake and the fire that followed. The church's exterior was restored and dressed in stone from the quarry in Gerakas. On May 10, the church celebrates the passage of the relics of Ag.

onto Dimokratias street which leads to the paved, triangular-shaped square of San Marco (Aghios Markos). Known in the old days as Platyphorus, since the end of the 16th century the square has been a meeting place for all the island's gentry. Every plebe who passed in front of the Bottega, the masters' coffee shop, was supposed to remove his or her hat and bow in a sign of respect to the ruling class. It was on this square, in 1797, that during the period of the French

A view over Aghios Markos square

Nikolaos. Around 1583, Ag. Dionysios, the island's patron saint, was a vicar at the church of Molos. During the feast of All Saints, in June, a fête is held at the temple. From Solomou square, turning left, we pass in front of the Greek Telecom (OTE) building and then

Democrats, the Popolari burnt the Libro d'Oro and symbolically planted the tree of freedom (see history on page 41).
Today, the very same square features a large number of tasteful and cosy restaurants and bars which, as the sun sets, turn the

Inside the Museum of Solomos

volume of their music up and lend a whole new tempo to the discussions of passers-by, couples and friends. The same square also features the church of Ag. Markos, established in 1518. Unfortunately both the passage of time and the devastating earthquakes that shook the island have taken their toll on the building, which nowadays lies desolate and stripped of all the works of art that once adorned its interior. The small garden opposite the catholic church of Ag. Markos once featured the Greek Casino, the Liberals' Club. Island authorities with the aid of the State have began the restoration of this historic building in the scope of reviving the old club in its original location.

The dials of the old clock situated next to the catholic temple since 1807, have patiently timed the passage of centuries gone by. At the start of the 1800 in place of the Museum of Solomos and Other Eminent Zakynthians, on San Marco's square, stood the church of the Pantocrator that was destroyed during the last earthquake.

The first to greet every visitor to the Museum is the statue of Dionysios Solomos, is actually is a replica of the original masterpiece by the sculptor G. Vroutsos, unfortunately destroyed during the 1953 earthquake. Upon entering, we cannot help but stop in front of the tree-trunk, under which Dionysios Solomos was inspired to compose the "Hymn to Liberty" and the "The Free Besieged". In the hall on the ground floor, in captivating lighting, we enter the Mausoleum of Kalvos and Solomos, at the end of which the museum exhibits the bust of our national poet. Kalvos' tomb bears the following inscribed verses from his poem the "Patriot":
"May my fate spare me
a tomb in foreign lands
death is sweet only,
when we rest in
our own country"
On the Museum's first floor we come across the halls of Nikolaos and Thaleia Kalyva, Alexandros and Dionysios Romas and the Illustrious

Inside the Museum of SolomΣs

Zakynthians, with finds from the life and work of these personalities. On the same floor, in the hall of Solomos the museum exhibits mementoes, portraits and personal belongings of our country's national poet.

The town's shopping street starts at the square of Ag. Markos and is at first called May 21st street, and later changes its name to Alexandrou Roma. Tertseti street, a parallel to May 21st street, in the direction of the hill, leads to Bochali and Tsilivi. The Court House along this street has a square in front of it, which features the statue of the jurist G. Tertsetis.

Behind the courts, Argasari street leads to the Old Fountain or Palaia Vrysi, which marks the beginning of the road that leads uphill to the church of Pikridiotissa, from which we may admire a scenic view of all the red-tiled roofs of the town below. An old path takes us from the church to the fortress. At the side of the church, a marble slab informs every visitor that the view of occupied Greece from this very spot was responsible for inspiring Kolokotronis to lead the War of Independence.

Returning downhill via Pikridiotissa street we end up at the beginning of May 21st street, at the point where the house of Dionysios Solomos used to be. At the corner with El. Venizelou street, we encounter the Town Hall of Zakynthos. The statues of Konstantinos Lomvardos and Alexandros Romas, members of the Ionian Parliament and significant personalities in the history of the island, stand before it. Opposite, under the archways, a collection of snack-bars and restaurants serving quick and simple food, succeed in attracting a large number of locals and foreigners every morning. Along A. Roma street, which

An oil-lamp in memory of Foskolos

features the characteristic array of arches which locals refer to as "kolones" (= columns), is the island's commercial centre. Over the shops, we have the chance to admire a group of carefully tended balconies, built in the style of the old town and decorated with colourful flowers.

Past the post office, we come across the temple of the Ascension or Analipseos, a three-aisle basilica dating back to the 16th century, with a castle-shaped bell-tower. In the same neighbourhood, along Foskolos street, we find the place where the home of the Greek-Italian poet, Nikolaos Oughos Foskolos lived. Nowadays, this very spot features a garden with a splendid statue of a lying angel, created by the Zakynthian sculptor Vitsaris. On the opposite corner, the small chapel whose oil-lamp still burns, is where, as the sign suggests, N. Foskolos used to read as a child. At the end of A. Roma street, we come across the square of Aghios Pavlos. The square is named after the church of Ag. Pavlos which was completely destroyed by the devastating earthquake, along with most other churches in town. At the small square, the street forks-out in two separate directions. Following Ag. Lazarou street, we exit the town in the direction of Volimes. Just

temple, among the other fine works of art, we can admire the icon of the Madonna bearing her child, which is given a procession in the evening of Easter Sunday. After the litany is over, a large fête is held with music, dancing and roast meat for every faithful worshipper.

Returning back to the junction on the square of Ag. Pavlos, we may then follow Kalvou street, which intersects a square named after it, and ends up on the main street

The impressive image of a bell-tower

before turning right to enter the main street to Volimes, we come across the temple of Volimes, which was built around 1500 and at first functioned as a monastery. For some time, the temple was run by Aghios Gerasimos, the patron Saint of Kefallonia. Upon entering the

leading to Laganas and the airport. Upon reaching the river of Ag. Lazaros, in the district of Giofyri, we take a left and travel along the river all the way to the beach road, the old Strata Marina, which is nowadays known as Lomvardou street. In the old days, the port road was the island's trading centre and housed the sultana warehouses along with the port's import-export depots. Currently, Strata Marina features restaurants, cafeterias, tourist gift-shops and most of the town's tourist agencies.

The paved square at the beginning of Lomvardou street features the most famous monument in Zakynthos: the temple of Ag. Dionysios, the island's patron Saint. Aghios Dionysios, who lived from Strofades. Later, on his way to the Holy Land, he passed through Athens where he was consecrated Bishop of Aegina. When later he became ill and decided to resume monastic life, he resigned his position as Bishop and spent the rest of his life in the monastery of Anaphonitria in Zakynthos (see 4th Tour).

Aghios Dionysios died on December 17 1624 in Strofades, where he was also buried. His relics were

the end of the 16th century to the beginning of the 17th, came from one of the island's aristocratic families, the Sigouros family, whose descendants were still inhabiting the island until very recently.

He spent the first years of his monastic life in the monastery on transported to Zakynthos some 100 years later, on August 24 1716. The entire island still celebrates both these dates with grand litanies and fêtes that succeed in attracting thousands of faithful worshipers.

The temple of Ag. Dionysios is amongst the very few buildings in

Zakynthos that was not destroyed by the recent earthquake. The three-aisle church was built in 1925 on the designs of professor Orlando. Externally, the church is known for its bell-tower which is very similar to the one of San Marco in Venice. The temple of the island's patron saint is lit at night and represents the symbol of Zakynthos; every visitor arriving to the island by night is captivated, as the church can be seen from afar with its gloriously lit bell-tower, resembling a significant landmark.

The Saint's relics are preserved in the church's interior, inside a silver-carved reliquary, created by the sculptors G. and D. Balafas. Glorious frescos created by Koutouzis and Doxaras, representing scenes from the Saint's life, adorn the temple's interior. The image of a litany in the women's pews in church along with the icon-screen carved in wood are quite spectacular. The monastery of Ag. Dionysios along with the monks' cells and a small ecclesiastic museum are located next to it.

The relationship between people from the Ionian and their various saints and patron saints is truly quite unique. They consider their saints as their very own fellow islanders, with faults and a human nature just like their own, and treat them accordingly. It's also quite impressive how these Ionian saints happen to be the children of some

Boat-loads of visitors by night

village families that have lived amongst common people for centuries. On many occasions, when they deem necessary, the Ionian people do not hesitate to complain about their saints and try to reason with them to their senses. However, whatever these islanders might choose to say about their saints, they will never hear anything bad from any foreigner.

During years of successive occupation, the people in the Ionian were severely pressured to follow Catholicism and, to survive, they had to develop this special relationship that brings man closer to God and fills him with unbelievable strength. The existence of tangible, local saints, as opposed to the intangible saints advocated by Catholicism, inspired strength in the islands' inhabitants and gave them the will to show faith in their own religion. This created the unique relationship between people and saints which characterises all the islands in the Ionian.

The church of Faneromeni (= the revealed) is situated a couple of blocks behind Ag. Dionysios and was built in the 15th century. Although severely affected by the earthquake in 1953, both the church and its bell-tower have been successfully restored. The square of Faneromeni, as opposed to the square of Ag. Markos which attracted the gentry, was the meeting place for common folk. Next to Ag. Dionysios is one of the town's older districts: Ammos had a beach which has long been land-filled to accommodate expansion. The small square that sits on its domain features the trees of Ammos, which include the trees of the Saint and the statue of Gr. Xenopoulos - the place where the home of the latter used to stand, nowadays features a small wood.

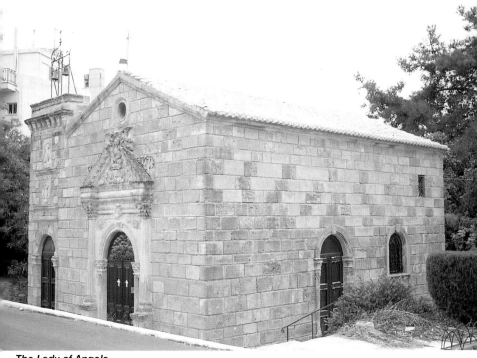

The Lady of Angels

We resume our walk through town and follow Lomvardou street towards the port. The intercity coach terminal is on El Venizelou street, one of the perpendicular streets along the way. A comprehensive coach service, connects almost every village and beach on the island and takes visitors to and from the mainland capital, Athens.

The small vessels that offer cruises around the island and call on some great beaches, the Blue Cave, and the small isles around Zakynthos, are moored along the port. Most such voyages depart around 9am and return at about 6pm, but schedules are often changed so we suggest you seek further information locally.

As we travel past Solomou square, the beach road that leads to the suburb of Kryoneri and Tsilivi, changes its name to Dionysiou Roma. On our left, through the town's narrow back-streets, we can

barely make-out the church of the Lady of Angels, built in 1687. To reach the temple, we need to go down a few steps. Its exterior is decorated with scenes carved into the church walls, while the rear courtyard features an old cistern. As we enter, we see three old tomb-stones at our feet, the icon-screen carved in wood before us, and the old icons that adorn the interior on each side.

Behind the church of the Lady of Angels - close to the square of Ag. Markos - we see the cathedral of Aghios Nikolaos "ton Xenon" (= of the foreigners). The temple was built on the rubble left behind by its predecessor after the devastating earthquake and was named after a local custom to bury the town's foreigners in its grounds.

Returning to the beach road we pass by the organised public beach, run by the Greek National Tourist Organisation (EOT), and then follow

The church of the Holy Trinity

the route that leads to Kryoneri, which takes us past the church of Aghia Triada (= Holy Trinity) with its castle-like, tall bell-tower. The church, built quite recently, has been decorated with the wooden carved icon-screen and the old icon of the Madonna of Laourentaina, which were transported from the temple of the Ag. Triada, situated within the castle walls.

The cemetery established in 1675 as a burial ground for the island's British inhabitants, is situated behind the temple. The individual

The old church of Estavromenos

graves feature tomb-stones made of marble from Gerakas, in the shape of temples. The area has been engraved in the memory of locals as the British cemetery.

As we approach Kryoneri, we pass by the small white chapel of Estavromenos (= Christ on the Cross), known from the 16th century. The old suburb of Kryoneri is famous for its taverns, great food, and its serenades, which feature the wholehearted passion of local singers.

BOCHALI - STRANI HILL

From the square of Ag. Markos we turn right towards Tertseti street and travel upwards along Filikon street to Bochali and the castle of medieval Zakynthos. Once we pass by the outdoor Town Theatre, we turn left towards the church of Ag. Georgios, built by the aristocratic Latinos family, but which has become known as the church of the Friendly or "ton Filikon". The white church seems whiter as it stands immersed in greenery and the shrubs that surround it. It was here, in Ag. Georgios, that the followers of the Friendly Society would be sworn-in - before the icon which is now on display at the Post-Byzantine Museum - amongst whom one recalls many famous heroes from the Greek War of Independence. On the right side of the icon-screen, a list bears witness to all those sworn-in within this church.

Resuming our tour we reach the intersection that leads to Bochali, villages in the plain, Strani Hill, and the promontory or Akrotiri (see 3rd Tour).

The left-hand-side branch leads to the hill of Bochali as it is called by the locals, the "outskirts of Bochali" or "exochoron" according to historians. The suburb, famous for its flowers and melon fields, is mentioned by notaries since the start of the 16th century. Bochali was characterised in those days by arched windmills, which existed from the early years of Venetian rule all the way to the period of British "protection". In fact, during the period of British rule, a large windmill called the "windmill of Begardakis" stood at the entrance to Bochali. The north-western corner of this Zakynthian medieval suburb, known then as the area of Arigos or Antilalos, was probably the site of the stadium of ancient Zakynthos. It was here that in the 18th century the statue resembling Apollo, Artemis and Aphrodite was discovered and is nowadays exhibited in the Tiepolo Museum in Venice.

The way the suburb of Bochali used to look in the old days, with its gardens and melon fields, was levelled during the earthquake in 1893 and every piece of its historical heritage eradicated. However, Bochali continues to represent a

pole of attraction for almost every visitor to Zakynthos, offering tourists a breathtaking view of the town and the surrounding areas. Its square features the church of the Madonna of Chrysopygi (= the source of life). Its interior is dominated by the gold-plated, wood-carved icon-screen and the icon of the Madonna which,

Inside the church of Aghios Georgios

Solomou square

The Lion of San Marco

A deserted fortress

aim their pointed roofs at the sky above, defying the threat of natural phenomena. The evenings in Bochali overflow with life and the sound of serenading flows from the taverns on the square and floods every street. The steep road in Bochali leads to the venetian fortress, whose ominous image and fortifications resembles many establishments of this type around Greece. As we cross the three consecutive gates, before entering the area where medieval Zakynthos used to exist, we cannot help but notice the Lion of San Marco, on the third gate, a symbol of its Venetian masters. Immersed in tall pine-trees, we can still make out the ruins of homes and once-famous old churches, which used to give life to the fortress. Nowadays, time has completed the destructive intentions of numerous earthquakes and the only buildings still left standing are the prisons and gun-powder rooms, with their railed-in windows. At the tallest point in the fortress, we are probably standing on the location of ancient Psofida. During one of the devastating earthquakes that changed the area's landscape, the fortress was separated from the neighbouring hill, Exintavelonis. Natural phenomena had hence succeeded in causing what the island's besiegers had striven for many years to achieve: i.e. the total destruction of the ancient capital's cyclopean walls. Even though the view from Bochali is somewhat suggestive, nonetheless the minute we reach the old fortifications we are captivated by the view that unfolds before our very eyes. Scopos, Laganas and out there the old fortress of Kyllini, and on the other side the castle of Aghios Georgios in Kefallonia! The view certifies the belief that the Venetian would select the location for their castles very

according to historians, bears the Byzantine numerals indicating its date as being 848 and the signature of the Byzantine hagiographer, Panisalkos.

The view from the hill is unbelievable as the town unravels before our feet and dips into the deep blue sea; the bell-towers of the churches below

The entrance to the old fortress

carefully, ensuring that they were always within view of eachother to enable communication in an emergency.

Opposite Bochali, as we take a right at the junction with the main road, we head towards the hill of Strani. We follow the paved path upwards until we reach the clearing from which we can see the island and the opposite shores. It is here that our national poet, Dionysios Solomos, sat and watched the developments during the siege of Mesologgi, which inspired him to write the great poem "The Free Besieged". Under an old oak tree, whose old and dried roots seem to have sprouted again - a piece of the original tree trunk is on display in the Museum of Solomos and other Eminent Zakynthians, in town (see page 86) - Dionysios Solomos wrote the "Hymn to Liberty". Certain verses from this very poem have become our country's National Anthem, set to music by Nikolaos Mantzaros, a musician from Corfu.

The peaceful atmosphere on the hill of Strani, seems to suggest that the poet's spirit is still wandering among the trees, captivated by the scenery, the tranquillity inspired by the view of Zakynthos below, the light as it shines through the olive-trees, and the deep blue sea in the background. The bust of Solomos erected on the paved clearing bears the great poet's verses:

"Nature is magic of beauty and charm beyond any dream
the black rock is all golden and the dried grass springs from a thousand fountains and speaks with a thousand tongues saying he who dies today will die a thousand times"
which seem to rise from deep within the spirit of everyone who happens to be standing, watching as the sun dips into the horizon, immersed in the peaceful and tranquil atmosphere of this very location.

The statue of Solomos on Strani hill

Tours

In all its beauty, Zakynthos can really baffle its visitors: its many beaches unique in their own way can make it very difficult to choose. The island, however is not only characterised by a captivating coastline. Its interior is thrilling as we visit picturesque villages built on hillsides offering an amphitheatrical view of the island below. People here have not changed much; they continue to live a simple life and are always willing to offer warm hospitality, treat strangers and greet visitors to their island with a smile.

1st TOUR
ZAKYNTHOS - ARGASI - VASILIKOS - GERAKAS

This route takes us to some of the most beguiling beaches, towards the cape of Gerakas, on the south-eastern tip of the island. Starting in the town of Zakynthos, we take Lomvardou street, the old Strata

The chapel of Aghios Charalambis

Marina, and follow signs to Vasilikos, which is about 17km from Zakynthos.

At the entrance to the town, immediately after the bridge over the river of Aghios Charalambis - the old Zakynthian suburb has been named after this - we encounter the small church of Ag. Charalambis, built in 1729 to honour the saint who saved the island from the plague. A stop at the church is well worth our time, the building that has been included in the island's archaeological monuments, features impressive exterior decorations, a gold-plated icon-screen carved in wood, and many rare icons in its interior.

A short while before we reach the town's old suburb, Argasi, we come across the old manor on our right, which after the establishment of the Friendly Society was the meeting place for all the "friendly" members. The suburb of Argasi, immersed in lush natural surroundings and in the shade of Mt. Skopos, is nowadays one of the island's cosmopolitan centres and succeeds in attracting many visitors from Greece and abroad. The road that cuts through the village is fringed on both sides by taverns, bars, hotels and rooms-to-let which, together with the endless crowds, lend it a truly lively spirit. The sandy beach which runs alongside the village is

ΖΑΚΥΝΘΟΣ
ZAKYNTHOS

ΑΡΓΑΣΙ
ARGASI

ΒΑΣΙΛΙΚΟΣ
BASILIKOS

GERAKAS BEACH

ideal for a swim close to town. The area surrounding Argasi is rich in churches, most of which are nowadays deserted as time and earthquakes proved to have had a stronger hand! We follow the main road through the village and soon come across a sign that directs us towards the ruins of a medieval tower.

As we leave Argasi behind, the road heads upwards and the beach spreads out before our feet. From this vantage-point we are able to see the thatched huts which the locals used to erect as shelters from the hot summer sun, for their early-afternoon siesta. The path leading to the peak of Mt. Skopos begins in Argasi. The ascent might be quite an exercise even for the very fit, but the view from the top is well worth it. Mythology states that Mt. Skopos was the home of the goddess of hunting, Artemis, and that the mountain was full of forests and temples.

The peak of Mt. Skopos currently features the deserted monastery of the Madonna of Skopiotissa, which was rebuilt in 1624, on the grounds of the sanctuary of Artemis. In the old days, the icon of the Madonna, which was brought from Constantinople, would protect the town from epidemics and pirates. "Panagia i Skopiotissa", the only church on Zakynthos with a cupola, has been built in a cross-like design and features many impressive frescos in its interior. Its major distinguishing element is its icon-screen which is made in stone as opposed to the other temples on the island, which have icon-screens carved in wood. They say that, on a clear day, the church is visible from every corner on the island.

Inside the chapel of Aghios Charalambis

The church of the Madonna Skopiotisa, on Mt. Skopos

The old bridge in Argasi

Descending through the path we have to stop once more to admire the view from Mt. Belvedere, as the Venetian called it. Further down, we gaze out onto the ruins of an arched bridge along the coast, built around 1885.

As we leave Argasi behind we promise to return for an excursion by-night and we come across a

sign that marks the boundaries of the area of Vasilikos. In reality, we don't come across the group of houses and buildings comprising a village, but merely small communities created after the devastating earthquake.

We return to the beach road once again, which climbs and gradually reveals a view of a lace-like coastline fringed with small houses and colourful gardens, and deluxe hotels built along the beach.

Although considerably developed over the past few years, Zakynthos still manages to retain the local spirit very much alive in its villages. Even in areas that experience a considerable tourist influx, behind the fancy bars and gift-shops we still find carefully preserved picturesque homes, with colourful, flower-clad gardens, just like the good old days on the island.

As we pass by Xirokastelo, about a kilometre later, on our right we come to the dirt-road leading to the beaches of Sekania and Daphne. Both Sekania and Daphne, beaches with rich sandy shores, are amongst the most significant breeding grounds for the Caretta-Caretta turtle.

Measures to protect the Caretta-Caretta turtle are in-force on both these beaches, as well as on most other beaches along the gulf of Laganas.

The egg-laying period for the Caretta-Caretta turtle lasts from June through August. The female of the species swim ashore at night, dig a nest in the sand, about half a metre deep, and lay their eggs. Some 60 days later, the young turtles begin their first trip towards the sea, usually at night. As stressed in the leaflets, which the Society for Turtle Protection on the island distributes to both

inhabitants and visitors, it is vital that the offspring succeed in reaching the water without human intervention, as scientists believe that this first trip is of vital importance to the survival of the species.

The members of the Society have placed signs along the beaches where egg-laying occurs informing the public about ways of protecting the turtle's nests. The beaches used for egg-laying along the gulf of Laganas are protected by special laws, and some have been declared Nature Reserves. The public is not allowed to be on

The beach of Porto Zoro

these beaches after sunset and before sunrise. On the beaches of Kalamaki and Laganas, with the exception of specially designated areas, no deck-chairs or umbrellas are allowed.

The Society's kiosk on the beach of Laganas distributes leaflets with more information regarding the ˙ Caretta-Caretta and the efforts of its members, along with local and private authorities, to establish a National Marine Park in Zakynthos. The Society's head office is situated in Zakynthos, on no. 1 Plessa street, opposite the Agricultural Bank.

We find ourselves once again on the main route leading to cape

The impressive Banana beach

Aghios Nikolaos and its church

Gerakas. No more than one kilometre from the intersection we were on previously, we turn left and follow the dirt-road leading to the picturesque beach of Porto Zoro, which features small, cosy taverns and a few rooms to let. The main road is intersected by small dirt-roads leading to virgin beaches and coves, most of which are deserted, untouched by tourism, sandy and ideal for all those who prefer quiet holidays away-from-it-all.

A few kilometres after Porto Zoro we come across the first sign for the Banana beach. This beach is so long that we eventually come across a second sign, which we follow and end up on its far side. With sandy tracks leading to it, Banana is considered to be one of the island's very best beaches and features a very wide sandy coastline and shallow waters. Thin, white water lilies grow on its sandy shores and lend it a somewhat exotic image. The lack of natural shade along this beach has led to the development of bars, offering their shade along with refreshments and light snacks, as well as the provision of a large number of beach umbrellas, which bathers are able to rent and protect themselves from the heat. Another choice in the same area is the beach of Aghios Nikolaos, which might be smaller and narrower than the Banana beach, but is just as beautiful. Floating jetties in the deep await the more daring bathers who wish to admire the cape of Gerakas in a parachute, dragged by a speedboat far, far below their feet. Those that are not inspired by the idea, may enjoy a whole range of different water-sports available, while speed enthusiasts can enjoy a ride on a range of jet-skis.

Picturesque Porto Roma
Mavratzis beach

Boats on calm waters

Gerakas, one of the most beautiful
beaches on Zakynthos

The small church of Aghios Nikolaos is situated in the left-hand-side of the beach; after the earthquake in 1894, the church was moved from its original location and built uphill on the rock. The right-hand-side of the beach is narrower and attracts fewer bathers, which makes it a favourite spot for those wanting to enjoy their swim in peace.

The road we were on up to this point, now forks-out in the direction of Porto Roma and the beach of Gerakas. The left branch of the road will take us to the beaches of Mavratzis and then to Porto Roma, which was named after the significant Zakynthian personality, Alexandros Romas, who had a house in the area. The picturesque beach of Porto Roma, which has a tarmac road leading to it, features crystal-clear waters and is ideal for a swim away from the crowds.

The dirt-road to Mavratzis leads to another great sandy beach, with clear light-blue waters. All those who get thirsty or begin to overheat may seek refuge at the open-air bar on the sand.

Once we pass through Vasilikos and by its blossoming gardens and picturesque taverns with their traditional serenading, we reach the beach of Gerakas, probably the best beach on Zakynthos. We abandon our car and walk the few metres that lead to the path descending to the beach. At the top of the path we have to stop for a few minutes to admire this glorious beach with its fine sandy shore and crystal-clear waters. The hot summer sun and its reflections make it impossible to distinguish the end.

As described earlier, Gerakas is one of the beaches preferred by the Caretta-Caretta turtle for its

When man and turtle meet

egg-laying process and the species has become the island's symbol of ecology. Both local inhabitants as well as foreigners feel it is their duty to protect the reproduction of these turtles, which are in danger of becoming extinct in the Mediterranean. Small wire meshes, scattered throughout the beach, protect small parts of the sandy shore, under which scientists and members of the Society have discovered and are monitoring new nests.

The left-hand-side of the beach is dominated by the impressive rock of the cape. A stroll all the way to the cape, through shrubs and beautiful flowers is well worth it. From the top of the promontory we can see the other beach of Gerakas, which is only accessible by boat, and opposite that we see the small, privately owned island of Pelouzo on which we make-out the remains of an old monastery.

2nd TOUR
ZAKYNTHOS - KALAMAKI - LAGANAS - AGALAS - KERI - KERI LAGOON

The second tour that we follow cuts across one of the island's most popular areas and ends in the cape of Marathias, and the Light-house in the village of Keri.

Leaving town, we head south following the sign to Kalamaki, which is about 8 kilometres down the road. Along the way we pass by picturesque churches, built amongst olives and cypress-trees, and scattered around the foot of Mt. Skopos.

Kalamaki is another of the island's tourist resorts. Its beautiful beach explains why this areas is a favourite amongst many visitors. On a windy day, the image of the beach is particularly impressive as its tall rocks along the side resist the force of the waves. The beach features a large patch which is covered by sand-dunes, "ammokoulouma" as the locals call it. During spring, this sandy patch is covered in water-lilies, whose fragrance is believed to travel far out at sea. The left-hand-side of the beach is dominated by an impressive formation of plaster rocks, the famous Gypsolithi or Ypsolithi.

As we leave Kalamaki we pass through Ambelokipi, where the island's airport is situated. We turn and follow signs to Laganas. The village's main road is fringed mostly by tourist gift-shops, restaurants, bars and generally anything that will cater for pleasant vacations. Behind the shops, deluxe hotels equipped with tennis courts and golf courses feature swimming-pools that try hard to compete with the inviting colour of the sea. Laganas has practically developed during the past few years, mainly thanks to tourism, and currently stands as one of the more densely populated areas on the island. A large portion of the island's visitors, mostly foreigners, use Laganas as a base for their trips around Zakynthos.

At the end of the road we reach the bay of Laganas, whose beach is over 9 kilometres long and features amongst the best of its kind in Greece. The entire stretch of the beach is covered by umbrellas and small bar-taverns, playing mostly foreign music, and creating a carefree and relaxing atmosphere from sunrise to sunset. (Don't forget that the beach of Laganas is subject to special laws for the protection of the Caretta-Caretta turtle.)

Small and makeshift canteens supply visitors with refreshing fruit salads, which tend to become increasingly in demand under the blazing sun. Sporting enthusiasts will find all they want on this beach. Its shallow, crystal-clear waters are ideal for fun and games, and its fine, sandy shore is welcome cushioning for tired bathers. The turtles, it seems, have made their choices very carefully and have selected the very best beaches around the island.

On the right-hand-side, opposite the beach of Laganas, we can see the small pine-clad isle of Ag. Sostis, named after the church which was once on its soil. The isle was part of the island's mainland until 1633, when it was separated by a powerful earthquake, and at present a bridge provides the most common means of access.

As the sun sets and the temperature begins to drop somewhat, we take advantage of the best time of the day to continue our trip through the south-eastern part of the island. We reach the main road once again and drive in

ΖΑΚΥΝΘΟΣ
ZAKYNTHOS

ΚΑΛΑΜΑΚΙ
KALAMAKI

ΛΑΓΑΝΑΣ
LAGANAS

ΑΓΑΛΑΣ
AGALAS

ΛΙΜΝΗ ΚΑΕΡΙΟΥ
LIMNI KERIOU

ΚΕΡΙ
KERI

Laganas by night

A Society's kiosk on Laganas

the direction of Keri. Along the way, we stop for a short while at the villages of Mouzaki and Pantokratoras. The road turns to Mouzaki and the island's old large village with its many springs comes into view. The village is adorned by the bell-towers that are still left standing and the local cathedral of Ag. Nikolaos, which was built in 1815 and has been recently restored. A short distance away, we come across the church of the Madonna, whose icon-screen features the carved date of 1741. As we approach the village of Pantokratoras, amongst the trees, we can distinguish the villa of Sarakina which, despite the passage of time and lack of care, still retains the red colour of its exterior walls and white finishings. Sarakina is a characteristic example of a Zakynthian manor and succeeds in exuding its grandeur to our days. Its name is tied to the past, when Saracen thieves would seek refuge on the hill and possibly within the villa itself.

The village of Pantokratoras is a very short while away and has developed under the "shade" of the old church of the Saviour (or Sotiras) or the Pantocrator, built on the mountain top. The free-form basilica of the Saviour, although aged through the passage of time, still manages to retain elements of Byzantine architecture. It is said that the church was built by empress Pulcheria during a visit to Zakynthos. A two-headed eagle dominates the floor of the temple's interior. The church's courtyard offers a view of the island's plain, the town of Zakynthos, and the deep blue sea of Laganas, offering visitors a few precious moments of relaxation and awe.

This entire area, with its old

The sea in Keri
The church of the Madonna in Mouzaki

The icon-screen of the Madonna

What's left of the manor of Sarakina

The old bell-tower of Faneromeni

Zakynthian villages built on the sides of the mountain with splendid natural surroundings, is ideal for walks amongst the trees, caves and small hidden churches that we meet along the way. The earthquakes in the island's past have destroyed a large portion of these villages and many have had to relocate on safer grounds. As we climb the hills and mountain-sides, we come across the ruins and remains of a side of the island that has long been washed away. However, the colourful scenery created by the flowers growing among the old rubble is a definite sign that life goes on, despite the adversities, on this beautiful Ionian island.

In fact, the island's inhabitants are probably the most optimistic of all, despite the destruction suffered throughout their distant and recent past. With great passion and care they carefully rebuild all that the force of nature has levelled on numerous occasions, while they raise their glass in local taverns and hum to the tune of old serenades in a clear indication of their undying spirit.

The village of Lithakia is one of the larger villages on the island, but the earthquakes and passage of time have long stripped it of all its architectural heritage. The village's church, Faneromeni, was built during the 14th century and like most churches on the island features an icon-screen carved in wood and many precious icons. Nowadays the church also displays icons that have been salvaged from other destroyed temples in the area.

From the village of Lithakia we deviate some 5 kilometres, in the direction of Volimes, in order to visit Agalas and the cave of Damianos. Agalas is a village that

Villages immersed in wild natural surroundings

The cave of Damianos
The area called the 12 wells or pigadia

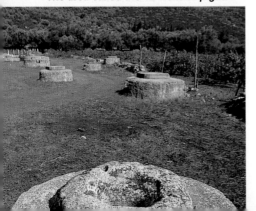

is built on the foot of a mountain, surrounded by pine-trees, on the island's western front. We cut across the village which features a few scattered homes and small cafeterias, and turn right following signs to the cave of Damianos. We pass through the old and almost deserted part of the village, with stone-built houses, leave the car in a clearing and follow the path downhill on foot. In a few minutes we reach the two-storey cave of Damianos, with its stalagmites and stalactites. A small gully before us, keeps us from the dirt-road on the other side of the mountain. We return to the village and follow the road in front of the Municipal building. Passing through vineyards we soon reach the area known as Twelve Wells or Dodeka Pigadia. The wells, which feature the island's traditional style, were built around the 15th century. From the Lighthouse of Keri, on cape Marathia, we are given the chance to witness one of the glorious Ionian sunsets. The quickest route to the Lighthouse, from where we stand, is the dirt-track which starts in Agalas and, cutting through hillsides with a variety of shrubs and trees, ends on the road to Keri. Our other option is to return the way we came and end up in Keri after passing by the Lagoon.

The idea to visit the Lagoon, once we have seen the sunset, and try some fresh fish in a tavern on its shore is quite appealing to us all. The sight of Keri from afar, asserts our suspicions that this village is quite different to what we've encountered so far. A short while before we actually enter the village, we come across the road leading to the site of the old and destroyed medieval village.

The main square in this small

village comes alive during the summer months with groups of locals and foreigners, who travel all this way just to admire the great view. The Madonna of Keri, or Panagia Keriotissa, is built on the clearing just below the village, where her icon was discovered. Locals claim that any effort to transport the icon proved futile, as it would miraculously return to its original location by night. The older generations take pride in describing how the icon had once-upon-a-time miraculously covered the village in dense fog, saving its inhabitants from the wrath of pirates. We travel along the narrow roads and reach the dirt-track leading to the edge of the cliff, and the Lighthouse that guides passing ships by night.

The lagoon in Keri

A sunset

The entire Ionian sea seems to lie at our feet: on the one side the vertical rocky sides of Marathias and on the other the steep sides of the hill, seem to complement the glorious colours of the sunset, creating a picture that we will find very hard to forget. As we leave, we are compelled to stop for a while at the small tavern which is at the very edge of the cliff and offers an unbeatable view of the rocks below, the Small and Large Myzithra or Mikri and Megali Myzithra as the locals call them. We leave the ever-changing colours of the sunset behind us and head for the Lagoon of Keri, the natural cove on the island's southern front. The area is known for its tar-springs, famous from the old days. At the entrance to the village we come across the "spring of Herodotus" with water that rises from deep in the earth's crust. On its far side we can still see the tar which the locals used to caulk their ships with in the past.

Along the relatively small bay of

The Madonna Keriotissa

115

Large and Small Myzithra

the Lagoon, small cosy taverns invite us to a different side of Zakynthos, perhaps somewhat less cosmopolitan, but nevertheless very picturesque. Despite current development, we are still able to savour fresh fish, local specialities, and roast rabbit and chicken accompanied by fine local wine.

From the Lagoon small boats take visitors on a tour of the caves along the sea-front, all the way to the impressive white rock, Small and Large Myzithra. The inhabitants of Keri have named the steep cliffs that dip into the white sands of Myzithra, Violantes. Our tour continues all the way to Marathias, which features impressive stone-arches and the isle of Marathonisi.

The older generations have a legend regarding this isle. Around 1500, the famous Peloponnesian soothsayer, Andreas Doxas lived on the isle. A Zakynthian, Ioannis Drakos, who went to seek his prophecies was warned by the soothsayer that his wife was planning to cheat on him. Wild with rage, the Zakynthian returned home and slaughtered his wife. The police that arrested both the murderer and the phoney soothsayer, sentenced them to death; the sentence was carried out on the isle of Marathonisi.

After their death, the inhabitants of the villages situated opposite the isle began to suffer from, as they believed, the appearance of an evil spirit that scared and haunted them. They began to believe that the soothsayer had cast a spell on the isle and the guards on cape Keri believed that it was the ghost of Doxas himself that had come to haunt their fellow villagers.

The island's governor was not convinced and dispatched his

The magic of nature meets Zakynthos

people to Marathonissi to investigate the strange phenomenon. They returned bringing the phoney ghost with them, who was none other than a smuggler who'd decided to make the isle his hide-out and exploited the fear of the villagers to serve his purpose.

A dirt-road that starts at the Lagoon takes us to the splendid pebble-beach of Marathias, with its crystal clear waters. This particular beach has many friends all over the island, who prefer it for the peace and tranquillity it inspires. On our departure we follow the road to Lithakia and travel across the gorge which is known as Abyss or Avyssos and was created by the earthquakes in 1633. At the far end of the gorge we discover a small natural spring with potable water and digestive properties, that empties into a small reservoir and flows into the stream of Kornos all the way to the sea. On

the mountain, above the gorge, we see the so-called Human Cave or Anthopini Spilia, which became the burial ground for 150 people, burnt to death in its interior by pirates.

On our return to Zakynthos we come across the narrow beach of Porto Koukla, with pebbles and grass that grows all the way to the sea.

The view to Porto Koukla

3rd TOUR
ZAKYNTHOS - TSILIVI - PLANOS - ALYKANAS - ALYKES

Although our third tour covers relatively short distances, it is nonetheless worth our while and deserves an entire day, in order to visit more than just one beach. Alykes, first and foremost, along with Tsilivi, Argasi and Laganas represent the most popular tourist destinations on Zakynthos. Our current route involves starting with a tour of the beaches along the island's northern reaches and returning through Zakynthos' interior, which will allow us a visit to the small villages built on the lush green hillsides of the island's mainland.

Driving along the old Strata Marina, currently known as Lomvardou street, we head towards Tsilivi. Driving past Solomou square and the public beach of EOT, we enter the suburb of Kryoneri, a short distance from

Venetian fountain in Kryoneri

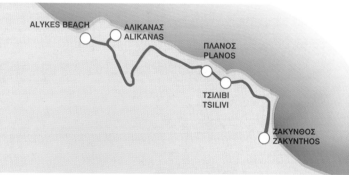

Zakynthos. Kryoneri (= Cold-water) owes its name to the spring which in Venetian times would supply passing ships with water. In fact, the stone-spring is still in its original location, facing the sea. The rock, which is behind the spring, on the opposite side of the road, is the one described in the novel by Grigorios Xenopoulos, entitled the "Red Rock" or "Kokkinos Vrachos".

Zakynthian manors

We reach the Cape a couple of kilometres outside town. This green and cool suburb was a favourite amongst the island's ruling class, who chose to build their country homes here. In fact the Solomos family also had a home here, nowadays belonging to the Chronopoulou family. The stone steps leading to its orange grove, represent its only link to its past. A few of the old manors have been restored and currently represent real gems, but most have been abandoned to the fate imposed by time and several devastating earthquakes, and all that remains of these is rubble.

Opposite the Cape, we see the isle of Vodi (= cow), which in the past was connected to the island's mainland by a small bridge. A number of explanations exist about the name of this particular isle. One theory supports that the isle was attributed the name because of the horn-shaped trees that grew on its soil. Another theory explains that the isle was given this name because of the cow that would lead the procession of the icon of the Madonna of Lavrentaina, as it was transported to the isle from the church in the fortress once a year. Another known name given to this isle is Triantaennea or Trenta Nove (= thirty-nine), which represents the number of Zakynthians executed by the Venetian on its soil, after demanding their political rights. In some documents, the isle is referred to as Fra Filippo, after the name of the hermit that used to live there.

The village of Tsilivi is a small settlement which is being continuously developed and features as a pole of attraction for a large number of visitors to the island. The short distance that separates it from Zakynthos, a mere 6 kilometres, along with its large sandy beach and surrounding green scenery, make it an ideal destination

Tsilivi by night

The beach of Alykes

for holidays combining entertainment and relaxation. The promontory of Toraditis or Gidakia shelters the gulf from the strong winds. An old Venetian watch tower, clearly weakened by time, still sits on top of the promontory. The northern winds, usually blowing in the area, make the local beach cool and pleasant even in the heart of the summer season.

The following village we encounter on our tour is the picturesque village of Planos, which as the years go by succeeds in attracting greater numbers of visitors. Swimming in this area is not a problem, as there are a number of beaches to choose from, some larger than others, but all sandy, with shallow waters and quite safe.

The main road leading to Alykes, a few hundred metres from the sea, takes us past areas that have already been successfully developed. In fact, this part of the island, along with the gulf of Laganas, succeeds in attracting most of the tourists on Zakynthos. On the other hand, in the north-western and western side of the island, the most scarcely populated areas on Zakynthos, we come across villages whose inhabitants are mostly farmers and livestock breeders.

Almost on every corner in Alykes we come across dirt-tracks and roads leading to secluded bays and beaches for all tastes. Some of the names that we see on street signs include Amboula, Pachyammos, Drosia, Psarrou and many more, which visitors will have to discover for themselves.

A couple of kilometres before Alykes, we reach the coastal settlement of Alykanas, an area of particular archaeological significance.

Excavations in Alykanas revealed Mycenaean vases, while in Pyrgos archaeologists discovered a destroyed vaulted tomb dating back to the same period. Both sets of finds, along with others in the surrounding areas, have led scientists to believe that this was the site of the ancient city of Arcadia. The highly picturesque beach of Ammoudi, in Alykanas, with its fine sandy shore, is the natural extension of the beach of Alykes. At the cape of Aghia Kyriaki, which divides the two neighbouring villages, we find the second beach of Alykanas and the beach of Aghia Kyriaki.

Picturesque beaches in Aghia Kyriaki

In Alykes, the gardens of restaurants and bars are bursting all summer long with large groups of people having great fun. The small river of Skourtis runs alongside the road and features a beautiful stone-built bridge, manufactured by the British during their possession of the island. The salt-pits, which in Greek are called Alykes and have lent their name to the village, are located behind the village and at one time were the most significant contributor to the island's economy. Alykes is also the home of one of the island's hot springs that has been given the strange name of "Kolosourtis", which loosely translated means "bottom-dragger"!

Alykanas

We leave Alykes and follow the road that brought us here, and turn right towards Gerakari to visit its three separate communities, Ano (= Upper), Meso (= Middle) and Kato (= Lower) Chorio (= Village). At Meso Gerakari we stop at the church of the Holy Trinity or Aghia Triada to admire its interior and the old icons that adorn it. After this, we set off on the road leading to Ano Gerakari. At the hill overlooking the village in an area called Anemodouri, we come across the church of Aghios Nikolaos. We decide to leave our car behind and climb the hill to the church which was once known as "ton xenon" (= foreigners'), as it was run by the local foreign parish. The view from up here is simply breathtaking, as the island's plain unfolds before us and we are able to admire the deep blue sea and the fortress in town.
On our return journey we cut across

123

the island's fertile plain. Both sides of the road are fringed with vast olive-groves, lending a silvery tone to the scenery, while the colourful flower-clad gardens in front of the houses meet make us turn our heads from side to side. As the road climbs upwards, the view which suddenly appears before us takes our breath away!

Before we reach Kalipado, we take some time to visit the villages of Kypseli and Tragaki, old Zakynthian villages whose inhabitants are mostly involved in olive production. Rumours on the island suggest that trees in Kypseli would bear fruit all year long, which is why the village was given its present-day name - Kypseli in Greek means Beehive. The windy roads leading to these two villages must be tackled cautiously, as their restricted width and sudden bends can take drivers by surprise.

When we reach the next village, Kalipado, we deviate past the old chapel of the Voultsos family. We then drive across the settlement of Chourchoulidio and the village of Vanato, take a left and end up at the hill of Bochali and from there in town where we began our tour.

The Zakynthian coast
The church of Aghios Nikolaos on the hill

4th TOUR ZAKYNTHOS - MACHAIRADO - LAGOPODO - KOILIOMENOS - AGHIOS LEONTAS - MARIES - PORTO VROMI - NAVAGIO - ANAFONITRIA

The western side of the island, from the cape of Schinari to Marathias, is the most scarcely populated part of Zakynthos. The coastline here is rocky and precipitous and, in most cases, inaccessible by land. The mountainous portion of the island is quite impressive thanks to its coastal formations; steep cliffs, small cosy bays usually accessible via narrow and steep foot-paths, and trees that seem to balance on the very edge, shedding their shade onto the crystal-clear waters far below. Archaeologists believe that, in the old days when the island's interior plains were no more than inaccessible swamplands, the inhabitants of this part of the island were forced to use these inaccessible coves to sail to neighbouring islands and the Peloponnese.

The villages we meet along the way are very different to the ones we visited in the plain. Smaller with narrow streets, seemingly hidden in the mountainsides, they give the impression of having been built in fear of pirate invasions. The sole exception to this theory being their tall bell-towers, which give-away their exact location, making our goal somewhat easier!

As nature begins to get ominously

The bell-tower of Aghia Mavra

denser, the road runs along the cliff of Mt. Vrachionas. Amongst the pine-trees we discover cypress-trees, lentisks, holly and many of the rare plants and shrubs growing on the island. Zakynthos is blessed by dense and highly varied natural surroundings, which keep it green and blooming all year long. Amongst the rare plants that we encounter, the island is known to boast some 42 different species of orchids and botanologists have called the area between Koiliomenos and Lagopodo

the "orchid garden".

Our trip across the villages in western Zakynthos begins, as always, in town. From May 21st street, on Ag. Markos square, we follow signs to Volimes. Some 3 kilometres later, we meet the intersection to Machairado. We turn and reach the village some 10 kilometres later.

The first few kilometres of our journey take us across the plain, cutting through fertile lands and colourful gardens. The road we're on seems pretty new, wide and a pleasure to drive on. This is naturally true only for the main route through the island, even though the deviations and side-streets that we are about to go on will not create any additional strain to our driver.

Machairado is the second largest village inland, after Katastari. On our approach we can clearly make-out the bell-tower of Aghia Mavra, which stands almost as tall as its surrounding trees, as if to indicate that the work of man can equal that of nature.

The church of Aghia Mavra houses the wonder-working icon of the saint, which is almost hidden behind the many offerings of its numerous worshipers. The church, featuring an impressive Venetian bell-tower, is built in the architectural style of a simple basilica, with a relatively standard exterior. Inhabitants claim, however, that its church-bells emit the sweetest sound and that when they ring they can be heard throughout Zakynthos.

In contrast to its plain exterior, the church is very impressive on the inside. Its gold-plated, wood-carved icon-screen is without a doubt the centre of attention. Famous artists and painters have contributed to the decoration of the church's interior; the frescos were created by Pelekasis, the glorious design on the ceiling was the work of Latsis, while

An impressive view inside Aghia Mavra

The monastery of the Madonna Eleftherotria

A carved icon-screen

Traditional Zakynthian well

The bell-tower of Aghios Nikolaos
Aghios Nikolaos in Koiliomenos

the women's pews at the far end, carved in wood and richly adorned, resemble a masterpiece of eastern art.

Every year, on May 3rd, during the fête of Aghia Mavra and Aghios Timotheos, the village attracts so many visitors that its feast is almost on a par with that of Aghios Dionysios. The feast is followed by a mass that lasts all night long. This particular feast succeeds in attracting worshippers by the thousands, not only from Zakynthos but from almost every corner of Greece.

Tradition has it that the icon of Aghia Mavra was discovered by a shepherd from the village of Lagopodo, on a fence. He tried in vain to remove the icon and take it to his village, but at night the icon would miraculously return to its original location, which is why the church eventually had to be built in that very spot.

The church of Ypapanti, is the other temple in the village, built in the 16th century, and whose bell-tower is amongst the tallest on the island.

On our way to Lagopodo we come across a view from above of the female monastery of the Madonna Liberator or Eleftherotrias, which although built recently, in 1961, was constructed in hewed stone which lends it an older look. The monastery, which looks like a fortress, offers a great view of Mt. Skopos and the fortress in Zakynthos. Its purple finishings contrast nicely with its otherwise white exterior and green surroundings, creating a truly unique picture.

Once we've crossed Lagopodo, we head in the direction of Koilomenos, at the entrance of which we encounter the small church of the Madonna. Its traditional stone-built bell-tower still retains some of the celestial-blue colour, which the locals had used when painting it in the past. The first name in the village was that of Aghios Nikolaos, after the name of the old church which still stands in its very centre. The restoration of the church's interior has already began and is expected to last a few years. As we enter, we are captivated by the icon-stand, which was recently gold plated, and the icon-screen carved in wood, whose impressive hagiographies and ornaments are done in dark red and green. Between the temple and its bell-tower, we have the chance to admire one of the many characteristic Zakynthian wells, which are quite common in villages throughout the island.

Directly opposite us stands the impressive castle-like bell-tower of Aghios Nikolaos which, according to the date inscribed on its step, was built in 1893. Its decoration is truly unique, as the structure is divided into floors, with round windows and a balcony where its bells are located. The absence of a roof, which apparently was never finished, lends a different tone to its highly impressive image.

In the village of Koilomenos, amongst many traditional homes, we come across a traditional eating-house called "Alitzerinoi", which according to a sign has operated since 1630. This traditional gastronomic establishment, housed inside an old home and divided into several small rooms on different levels, often gathers a large number of locals. From Koilomenos we drive along the

Traditional eating-house

The Monastery of the Madonna Yperagathou

dirt-road that takes to the coast. As we cut across ploughed fields and stone walls, we are suddenly surprised by a view from above of the isle of Korakonisi (= crow island). The edge of the isle is characterised by a square hole, which seems manmade. Apparently, during winter and when the sea gets rough, the water enters the hole and is propelled high into the air.

The wind has become somewhat cooler, reminding us that we stand some 500 metres above sea-level. The route we follow is different to the fields and olive-groves, which we had grown accustomed to so far, and keeps us constantly alert. With Koilomenos far behind us now, we follow the country lane leading to the Monastery of the Sublime Madonna or Yperagathou, built on the side of the mountain, close to the peak called Atheras. The entrance to the small and deserted monastery is

Ruins of an old gem

dominated by a hewed water basin, one of the largest of its kind on the island.

Once on the main road again, we follow the sign to Aghios Leontas, named after its church which was built in the 14th century.

No more than one kilometre before entering the village we turn at the cross-roads and head towards the most mountainous villages in Zakynthos, Loucha and Gyri. The four-kilometre drive to Loucha goes by in a flash, as all of us are captivated by the great sea-view to one side. We can see the water through the pines and at the far end we can make out the cross of Schiza. These two mountain villages are practically buried in greenery and their small stone houses, with light yellow and red tiled roofs, remind us of other parts of Greece. In fact, as the locals testify, the first inhabitants of Loucha came from Mani in the Peloponnese and built their homes

Daily life on the island

according to the architectural style of their homeland. As we approach Loucha, at the entrance to the village we see the ruins of a windmill and the local farmers watching over their crops from traditional thatched huts. The road continues towards Gyri, built at an altitude of some 550 metres and known from the 15th century. The village square features the church of Profitis Ilias, rebuilt by the inhabitants after the devastating earthquake. The stone-built houses in the village are small and the streets narrow, making it very difficult to

Traditional thatched hut in Loucha

travel by car. Inhabitants are mostly farmers and cattle-breeders, but one can also find sculptors that work with the soft rock found in this part of the island. Even though this is definitely the most mountainous village on Zakynthos, tourism is not new in the area and as we walk through its narrow back-streets we come across a sign that says "Coffee Shop and Beer"!

A road that starts in Gyri leads to the cave of Chagiotis and the so-called Black Cave or Mavri Spilia, at an altitude of 615 metres. All we know about the cave of Chagiotis is that it has three sections with stalagmites and stalactites, and that it is still unexplored.

We head back to the intersection with the main road and enter the traditional village of Aghios Leontas. A visit to the village's church built in memory of the old bishop from Catania on Sicily is well worth our while. It is here, in fact, that we are convinced of the inexhaustible creativity of local architects, as we discover that the lower part of an old windmill has been converted into the church's bell-tower! In the very heart of winter, on February 20th, the village celebrates the memory of its patron saint. Weather permitting, the villagers hold a procession of the icon through the village, otherwise the service is held inside the church. The main street through the village is often coloured with rugs and hand-woven products sold by locals in small traditional shops. From the village we follow the road to Limionas. This beguiling bay, where rocks eroded by sea and time have created small pools, features a small cosy beach on its far end. The blue narrow patch of water that washes its shore resembles a fjord, while the pines bow over the water in a sign of respect to this amazing combination! The entire area is so beautiful that we

were not in the least surprised to encounter the first telltale signs of future tourist development.

The numerous windmills encountered along the way remind us of the not-too-distant agricultural past of the area. People here used to lead simple lives and depended on the land for survival. Even though both life and needs have changed a lot since then, the area still has a number of inhabitants who continue to live off farming.

We return to the main road and Aghios Leontas, and set off for our next destination, which is the village of Kambi, built on the foot of the steep rock of Schiza. A large stone cross dominates the top of the rock, a monument built in memory of those who lost their lives here during the years of occupation. Directly opposite, the island of Fokia (= seal), named because of its resemblance to the cute mammal.

As we climb the rock we come across

High on Schiza

the Mycenaean graveyard with its hewed tombs, which unfortunately have been stripped of their belongings. Excavations in the area have proved that there are many more secrets regarding the island's interesting past which are still well hidden.

The sunset at Schiza is definitely one of the best in the Ionian. Small

Mycenaean burial grounds

cafeterias built on the side of the rocks allow us a few precious moments of relaxation, accompanied by a glass of local wine.

After Kambi, we turn left and head to Exo Chora, a small village whose houses seem to have survived the earthquakes that shook the island. The village's church, Aghios Nikolaos, is decorated by an icon-screen, dating back to 1700, and many valuable icons. In the village we are able to ask for directions to the strange geological phenomenon of Kato Lakkos (= lower pit). This particular spot reveals a piece of earth, at a depth of 30 metres, which is enclosed by very steep rock and the most logical explanation is that this was once a cave whose roof collapsed.

The next village on our itinerary, Maries, owes its name to Mary Magdalene and Mary the Wife of Clopas, who according to tradition were the first to introduce Christianity to the island. Tradition in fact has it that they were on their way to Rome to protest about the crucifixion of Jesus, when they stopped in Zakynthos. In the bay of Porto Vromis, the locals show us the footprint left by Mary Magdalene on a rock, as she set foot on the island. In the village, the old stone homes still manage to blend in peacefully with newer ones. As we walk through the village, we can't help noticing the traditional Zakynthian wells, some in natural stone tints and others painted in lively colours.

In the interior of the three-aisle church of Mary Magdalene, built in the 15th century, we stand and admire the traditional icon-screen and the stone cross. On July 22nd the village celebrates in memory of Mary Magdalene, stages a procession of the icon, and holds a large fête. The village of Maries also celebrates the feast of Aghios Charalambous, on

Tempting waters in Schiza

Homes painted in the Ionian colours in Exo Chora

The temple of Aghios Ioannis in Machairado

**Inside the church
of Mary Magdalene**

**The church in Maries
Beguiling Porto Vromi**

February 10th, who saved the village from the plague. On the dirt-road towards the bay of Stenitis we come across the ruins of the medieval church of Aghios Charalambis. At Stenitis we notice from above that the crystal-clear waters allow us a clear view of the sea bed below!

From the village of Maries we are able to follow yet another dirt-road, which after about an hour's drive will take us to the top of Mt. Vrachionas. Those that are not afraid to take on some exercise will be rewarded by the breathtaking view. The Ionian spreads beneath our feet and the sea changes from a bluish-green tint to dark blue as our view from this point is unrestricted all the way to Kefallonia. The famous Shipwreck, one of the most photographed beaches on Zakynthos and probably the most beguiling in Greece, is now only a breath away.

To reach the famous beach of Aghios Georgios, known as the Shipwreck, we can follow the signs from Maries or from the village of Anafonitria, which we shall visit later on. As soon as we enter the village of Maries we follow signs which lead us onto a relatively wide road, which takes us to Porto Vromi a few kilometres later. The waters in Porto Vromi are clear and inviting, and many visitors rent pedalos or small boats, which are ideal for exploring the neighbouring sea-side caves. The small harbour here is the starting point for small vessels that carry tourists to and from the famous Shipwreck every hour. If you decide to go on this short journey, make sure you take plenty of water with you.

The boat trip lasts about half an hour. The captain stops at caves with crystal waters and white sands, and those wanting to swim may do so. The lime-stone and water reflections lend the sea below an impressive shade of blue. Before we reach the

Shipwreck, we pass by another two small idyllic coves, ideal for those who enjoy swimming alone. Access to these is only possible by private yacht or upon agreement with the captain, who will drop you off and pick you up on the way back.

As we turn into the bay of Aghios Georgios, as the Shipwreck is officially called, we finally meet the famous beach with the thick white sandy shore. The corroded shipwreck in the middle makes the picture even more impressive, while the vertical rocky cliffs surrounding it make this beach something truly extraordinary. Every summer this particular beach, which along with the Caretta-Caretta turtle have become the island's trademark, is visited and photographed by thousands of tourists. Thankfully though, despite the crowds which one may encounter here on some occasions, the beach is kept clean and its charm is carefully preserved.

If we do not head towards Porto Vromi from the village of Maries, then on our way to Anafonitria we come across a second road leading to the Shipwreck and ending on the right-hand-side of Porto Vromi.

The village of Anafonitria - otherwise known as Plemonaria (a variation of the phrase "to the monastery") or Prosmonario (a variation of the phrase "in front of the monastery") - is only 4 kilometres from Maries. We take the dirt-road from the village and reach the monastery of Aghios Georgios of Krimnes, which in the old days was built on the very edge of the cliff.

The monastery was built around 1540 by the abbot Varlaam Beletis. The monastery must have known fame and glory in the past and it is said that it used to feature an extensive library. This is where the patron saint of Kefallonia, Aghios Gerasimos, lived the life of a recluse. We follow the path leading to a small clearing below the monastery and come across the cave that was the saint's hermitage. In fact, it was here, in this very monastery that the theologist and historian, Pachomios Rousanos, wrote the largest portion of his work; his grave is in the monastery's courtyard.

During the monastery's eventful past it was attacked by pirates on several occasions and suffered severe looting and destruction. The monks however, steadfast in their faith and armed with inexhaustible supplies of patience and perseverance, would repair or rebuild their monastery accordingly. On one of these many occasions, erosion forced them to rebuild somewhere safer, where the monastery stands today.

The dirt-road we followed from Aghios Georgios, takes us about a kilometre later high on the rocks to a place that offers us a breathtaking

Sunset in Porto Vromi

view from above of the famous Shipwreck and the amazing work of nature.

We return to the village with the image of the shipwreck imprinted in our minds and take the dirt-road leading to the monastery of the Madonna of Anafonitria. They say that, during the fall of Constantinople, a cargo vessel from that city had sunk just off Zakynthos. The locals that found the icon of the Madonna bearing her child or "tis Vrefokratousas" among the rocks, built the country church and later the monastery in that same location. They also say that at the spot where the icon was discovered, there was a strange flickering light as if the icon itself were crying out, which is why they attributed the name Anafonitria (= she who cries out).

The monastery of the Madonna of Anafonitria was built during the 15th century and represents one of the eight monasteries on the island to have survived the devastating earthquake in 1953. The nave of the church is a three-aisle basilica with a wooden roof and represents a unique exception in Zakynthian architecture along with the church of Skopiotissa. Its interior still features impressive frescos and the old icon-screen, which has

**The monastery of
the Madonna Anafonitria**

darkened with time. The two-headed eagle can still be seen dominating the church's floor. The chapel of Aghia Anastasia is located within the monastery.

The courtyard is dominated by the bell-tower, a vertical castle-like structure with six loopholes used for pouring hot water or oil. In fact most of the bell-towers in the area used to act as look-out posts, from which the monks could monitor a large portion of the land surrounding the monastery. In the unpleasant event of pirate attack, these bell-towers would serve as the final refuge for the monks.

One of the abbots in Anafonitria was the island's patron saint, Aghios Dionysios. They also say that at some stage his brother's murderer sought refuge in this very monastery. Even though Aghios Dionysios realised who this man was, he helped him escape through Porto Vromi to Kefallonia. The saint's cell is located in the monastery's courtyard, where his personal effects and vestments are still preserved.

The icon of the Madonna of Anafonitria is considered to having wonder-working abilities. In the old days, in fact, locals used to stage a procession of the icon during times of drought hoping it would bring rain. The fête of the Madonna of Anafonitria is held a week after that of Aghios Dionysios and succeeds in gathering many worshippers from every part of the island.

Leaving the village of Anafonitria, at the end of a long and thoroughly enjoyable day, we have many return routes to choose from. We can go back the way we came from or pass by Orthonies and visit the villages of Riza and drive along the foot of the mountain back to town (we shall get to know this route during our 5th Tour).

The monastery of Aghios Georgios of Krimnes

5th TOUR
ZAKYNTHOS - RIZA VILLAGES - KATASTARI - AGHIOS DIMITRIOS - AGHIOS KIRYKOS - SARAKINADO - ZAKYNTHOS

The fifth tour we propose runs along the foot of Mt. Vrachionas and ends back in town via the island's plain. During this route the greatly varying scenery will surprise us on many occasions. Along the way we come across small villages, rooted into the mountainsides, houses practically hidden in olive-groves, tall trees, old and recent churches. The devastating earthquake did not spare the efforts of people living in town or in the country and many villages were totally wiped-out, but their inhabitants have mastered the will to rebuild all that has been destroyed and save their home-lands from desolation.

Villagers here are usually farmers growing olives and vines, the latter producing the famous Zakynthian wine. In the countryside we come across many groves and farms, while in August, the side of the road is fringed by sultanas, the produce that once upon a time was a major contributor to the island's economic prosperity.

As we leave town, we follow the road to Machairado which, apart from the church of Aghia Mavra, is also quite famous for its souvlaki (= kebabs). At the centre of the village we will

ΚΑΤΑΣΤΑΡΙ
KATASTARI

ΑΓ. ΔΗΜΗΤΡΙΟΣ
AG. DIMITRIOS

ΑΓ. ΚΗΡΥΚΟΣ
AG. KIRIKOS

ΣΑΡΑΚΗΝΑΔΟ
SARAKINADO

ΖΑΚΥΝΘΟΣ
ZAKYNTHOS

Sultanas, one of the island's main products

turn right towards the villages of Vougiato and Langadakia. A short while after Machairado we drive through the settlement of Melinado. This is where the ruins of the church of Aghios Dimitrios, marble columns and a slab bearing an inscription in Doric were discovered, the latter deriving from the ancient temple of Artemis Opitaida. Historians believe that this temple was located in the area around the village of Vougiato. At Vougiato we come across the church of the Madonna, featuring an impressive gold-plated wood-carved icon-screen and wooden mesh in the women's pews. Along the road behind the church we come across the temple of Aghios Ioannis Theologos (= divine), which was built on the ruins of the ancient temple of Artemis Opitaida. We go back a short while and upon crossing the main road enter the area of Langadakia. The surrounding scenery is dominated by olive-groves and sultana plantations. The road from Langadakia leads back to Zakynthos through the plain. In the centre of the village we see the church of the Divine Virgin Mary or Yperagias Theotokou with an impressive icon-screen and hagiographies.

Directly opposite, we see the dirt road that heads towards the old village, high up on the mountainside, which was abandoned after the earthquakes. We can drive to that old settlement by car, provided we take great care with the pot-holes on the way. Amongst the rubble, we make-out only scarce signs of life and the destroyed bell-towers that used to bless the village with their sound. We drive back to the main road unable to see the plain through the thick olive-groves beside us.

The parish church in the village of Fiolitis is adorned by an impressive stone-built bell-tower. Its interior now displays an interesting collection of icons and wooden objects from the older churches in the village, including Aghios Nikolaos of Schinas and the Madonna of Fiolitis. In fact, it is quite a common feature across the island to visit churches that preserve the effects and icons from other churches that have perished in the devastating earthquakes. As we travel across the village of Fiolitis, its

The church of Aghia Marina

The glorious centre decoration of Aghia Marina

small traditional shops take us back several decades.

The villages of Riza are built next to eachother almost in a straight line. The main road usually takes us past the parish church of every village. On both sides of the road we see houses, in most cases hidden within the surrounding fields to serve the purpose of their inhabitants' agricultural and farming lifestyle. About a kilometre from Fiolitis we come across Galaros and, after the bend, we meet the village of Aghioi Pantes (= All Saints).

Just before entering the village, we come across the steep road leading to the church of Vlacherena. We decide to take this road even though it is not paved and, despite the steep climb, the end result is well worth our while. The church of Vlacherena is barely visible through its dense natural surroundings, while a few metres further up we see the reservoir that supplies the surrounding villages with water from a well.

Back onto the main road we take a left this time towards the village of Aghioi Pantes, which was named after its church, built in the clearing on the foot of the mountain. The surrounding scenery is mountainous and the reddish rocks around us shelter the village in their shade. Further up the mountainside we can see the village of Aghia Marina of Fagia, a name it took from one of the families that lived in it in the past. As we ascend the narrow lane leading to the village's church we arrive at the foot of the mountain, where we can admire the picturesque bell-tower of Aghia Marina. For many years now, both the church and its surrounding quarters have been declared historical buildings.

The church's courtyard features the old village school, which represents

147

The chain in Aghia Marina's cell

a prime example of Zakynthian architecture. On the other end we can still see the small square cell in which the locals would lock-up the insane from every part of the island. The older generation recall that at times there were so many insane to accommodate and because the cell was so small, they had to tie many of them on the trees in the church's courtyard. Inside the cell we can still see the thick chain they used to tie-up their insane prisoners. Before the cell was built, the chain and securing boulder were placed behind the church, where the insane would be chained in the hope that Aghia Marina would cure them.

The church of Aghia Marina that we can visit today was built in 1855 over the old temple which dated back to 1643. In fact, the old church was built in a different style from the one we see today, and featured a narthex or porch and the village's burial ground

in its courtyard.

The present-day crucifix-shaped temple was constructed in stages. Its corner-stone was laid in 1855 by the engineer D. Feradouros, from the neighbouring village of Machairado, and was completed in 1874. The wood-carved icon-screen in its interior belonged to its predecessor. The Madonna on the icon-screen, which dates back to 1680, was created by G. Vidalis. The church's interior is adorned by eight domineering single-cast stone columns, about 6 metres tall and 1.85 metres in diameter. The columns were carved out of a single rock, discovered in 1855 in the area of Koutoufaris, in the location of Batisteika.

The bell-tower, which had collapsed in the earthquake, was reconstructed by local engineers who used the original stones and materials, as much as possible, and succeeded in recreating its original shape and decoration. We ascend the windy staircase and are offered a view from above that is truly breathtaking. From the bell-tower we are able to see the plain and gulf of Alykes.

Our friendly chat about Aghia Marina with the locals reaches an end and we set off for the village of Skoulikado via the settlement of Drakas. The church of Aghios Dimitrios that we meet along the way, features an interesting and precious collection of icons and other ecclesiastical objects from older churches around the area. The church's interior is adorned in stone-carved decorations, while its impressive Zakynthian bell-tower is serviced by a narrow staircase in its interior.

The trip through the villages of Riza is a real pleasure. The small and large homes that we come across are all fringed with colourful and carefully tended gardens. The courtyards are

Images forgotten in time

full of vines and fruit-laden trees, groves and plantations stretch out as far as the eye can see, and their inhabitants friendly and helpful, depict the true picture of this unique island.

In the village of Skoulikado we come across the church of the Madonna Anafonitria, which is built on a natural ledge overlooking the plain. Its impressive bell-tower rises some 34 metres upwards, indicating the exact location of the village.

At the edge of the village we stop at the church of Aghios Nikolaos Megalomatis (= broad-eyed). The entrance to the church's courtyard is through the archway of its stone-built bell-tower. As we enter the temple, we come across the imprinted image of Aghios Nikolaos on the floor, next to the icon-screen. Legend has it that the image was found and that the only human touch supplied was the silver frame surrounding the icon. The area also features to hot natural springs, Magera and Gremna.

Skoulikado is amongst the island's villages that boasts a rich cultural heritage, both with respect to religion and arts. In fact, the village's cultural society organises regular Discourses/Dialogues throughout the entire year.

Our route continues alongside the foot of the mountain and takes us to the villages of Kallithea and Pigadakia. The village of Kallithea or Koukesi, spreads out on both sides of the road and features an abundance of olive-groves. Kallithea is also home to the Magkioros spring, which is famous for its natural mineral water.

Opposite the church of the Madonna or Enomenon Naon (= united temples) - which currently houses icons and precious artefacts from older churches in the village - we come across the dirt-road leading to the old village, nowadays deserted

following the earthquake's destructive force. As we ascend, the glorious view of the plain below us seems like an expensive painting. This in fact is the road leading to the so-called Black Cave and the village of Gyri, which we visited during our 4th Tour.

Our next stop is the village of Pigadakia, another village built on the foot of the mountain, and which has been named after the old sulphur springs that existed in the area. Legend has it that the water from the well situated under the altar, in the church of Aghios Panteleimon, is "stirred" during the feast of the saint and that worshippers take this instead of holy water.

The parish church of Aghia Varvara in the village is the home of icons and ecclesiastical treasures rescued from churches in the area that were destroyed in the earthquakes, among which the churches of Vlacheraina

A church in Katastari

and Aghios Ioannis Theologos. We leave the village of Pigadakia behind and set off for the most densely populated village on the island, Katastari. The largest portion of this village is built in an amphitheatrical fashion, on the side of the hill, overlooking the gulf of Alykes. Once again, the church of Aghioi Theodoroi has become the home of portions of icon-screens and valuable decorations as well as the personal effects of old neighbouring temples, which have perished long ago. The village of Katastari is known for its great musical heritage. In fact, the village features its own philharmonic, which accompanies local processions and fêtes.

From the old village, higher up the hillside, we can see a very large portion of the island's plain. Its is quite amazing how the imagination of the Zakynthians over the years has created names for every hillock and valley that we meet along the way. Some of the names attributed actually originate somewhere in the island's eventful history and others are just the fiction of folk imagination. The area at the far end of our view, close to the village of Gerakari, is where the spring of Vromoneri is situated; the vapours it expels are known to relieve rheumatism.

A number of cement footpaths leading to Alykes begin from the main road through Katastari. We follow these and come across a number of tourists who take a stroll through the splendid natural surroundings in the area.

The gulf of Alykes offers visitors a great deal of choice in the way of swimming. Its beaches, some more crowded than others, are all blessed with sandy shores and are ideal for a quick revitalising dip before we continue our journey. On our way back to Zakynthos we pass by villages in the plain which, in the old

The church of Aghios Kyrikas

days, were amongst the wealthiest on the island thanks to their location. The next settlement on our itinerary is called Aghios Dimitrios and features, naturally, a church of its patron saint. Its small, white-washed houses and the sultanas lying on both sides of the road, create an eye-pleasing picture. On our way towards Aghios Kirykas, on our left, we come across the small obelisk, a monument to the patriots who lost their lives in the fight for freedom during the Second World War. The church of Aghios Kirykas, built recently before the earthquake, is situated along the main road in the small square in the village. On July 15th, the village stages a traditional fête and feast in memory of its patron saint.

Sarakinado, which we meet just a few kilometres before town, features a few deserted homes still left standing after the devastating earthquakes, on which we discover traces of the village's long lost past. In the square, we visit the parish church of Aghios Nikolaos, whose interior is adorned by the icon-screen from the church of Aghios Ioannis Prodromos (= John the Baptist) which used to be in the fortress. As we leave Sarakinado behind us, we drive along the harbour on our way back to Zakynthos.

KOPIΘION
KORITHION

ΑΓ. ΝΙΚΟΛΑΟΣ
AG. NIKOLAOS

MAKRIS GIALOS BEACH

ΒΟΛΙΜΑΙ
VOLIME

ΟΡΘΟΝΙΑΙ
ORTHONIE

ΖΑΚΥΝΘΟΣ
ZAKYNTHOS

6th TOUR
ZAKYNTHOS - ORTHONIES - VOLIMES - KORITHI - AGHIOS NIKOLAOS - MAKRYS GIALOS

Our 6th Tour takes us to Zakynthos' north-western side, where wild natural surroundings and steep rocky cliffs comprise yet another beguiling picture of this highly interesting island. The route we shall follow towards Orthonies will take us once again past the cosmopolitan beaches of Tsilivi, Alykanas, Alykes and then to the ascent of Mt.

Vrachionas with a great view of the gulf of Alykes below. This route allows us another chance to admire the crystal-clear waters around Zakynthos and its colourful sea-bed. The cape of Schinari is the island's most northern tip and the closest point to the island of Kefallonia. In fact, small boats set off from the harbour of Aghios Nikolaos and take visitors across the two neighbouring islands. Although the tour we recommend covers a distance of some 45-50 kilometres, it is well worth your while and should be

Zakynthian beaches

allocated an entire day. The large new section of the road and charm of the scenery we cross will reward us for our decision.

We pass by Alykes and follow the wide, new road towards the mountain village of Orthonies. A few kilometres later, we come to the dirt-road leading to the monastery of Aghios Ioannis Prodromos (= John the Baptist), which was built during the 16th century. Amongst the old and long-deserted cells we meet the single-aisle basilica, whose interior is still adorned with fine examples of ecclesiastical art, such as the icon-screen and the icon depicting the decapitation of John the Baptist. The old stone, traditional bell-tower supports the cross and raises it triumphantly towards the heavens above, while the panoramic view includes the island of Kefallonia and the mountains in the Peloponnese. We return to the main road in the direction of Orthonies. Along the way, we will come across the intersection leading to Maries, from which we can take a boat-ride to the famous Shipwreck. Orthonies is a village which is built in an amphitheatrical fashion on the side of Mt. Vrachionas, featuring stone houses with tiled roofs in colourful red and pale shades. The main square features the church of the Archangels Gabriel and Michael, which is decorated with an old wood-carved icon-screen and a number of impressive icons.

About a kilometre down the road, we come across the monastery of the Madonna Spiliotissa (= from the cave), which was established in the 16th century. The monastery was named after the icon of the Madonna was found in a cave on the opposite side of the mountain. The monastery's church is a three-aisle basilica surrounded by auxiliary quarters.

The route that takes us to the monastery continues to the area of Koroni, cutting through hills whose predominant characteristic are bare rocks and limited vegetation, until we finally reach the coast. This is where the sulphur springs in the area shed their waters. The high sulphur contents of these waters create white clouds in the sea below. The area, called Xygkia features a small and somewhat inaccessible beach which, nevertheless, is very picturesque and one of the best in this part of the island.

From Koroni, a new road takes us to Makrys Gialos. Actually, at the time of writing, the road is still under construction, but hopefully will be ready and fully operational by summer 1996, making touring this part of the island a whole lot easier. We rejoin the main road in the direction of Volimes, pass by

The monastery of Spiliotissa

A world full of colour

Orthonies and at the cross-roads we take a right towards Volimes. The road begins to climb and after a bend we encounter the stone homes of the village, in complete harmony to the wild surrounding scenery. Before we actually enter the village we come across the colourful local hand-woven creations, displayed on fences along the way. In fact, Volimes is quite famous for its fine hand-woven products and the lace created by the women of the Agricultural Co-operative. Along the road, we also see villagers selling local oil-cheese, wine and honey. The village of Volimes is in practice made up of three separate communities, the Ano (= upper), Kato (= lower) and Meso (= middle) Volimes. Through the neatly white-washed houses and courtyards with vines, we can make out the church of Aghia Paraskevi, which dates back to 1633. The church's bell-tower is an exact replica of that of

Traditional hand-woven products in Volimes

the church of Aghios Dionysios in town.

A few years ago, the parish of Volimes established the Women's Co-operative for Country Tourism, which rents rooms to people wishing to get to know the area and visit its environs. This is also an excellent opportunity for the town-folk wishing to come closer to nature and learn more about local agricultural activities.

From Meso Volimes we take the road leading to the cape of Schinari and the so-called Blue Cave. We can see the church of Aghios Spyridonas dominating the community in Kato Volimes. Although weathered by time, the church's bell-tower continues to raise its red-coloured cupola towards the sky.

As we leave Kato Volimes we head towards the deserted monastery of Aghios Andreas, built on the very edge of the cliff. The frescos that once adorned its interior are currently on display in the Museum of Post-Byzantine Art in Zakynthos. The view from this point is simply captivating. Below us we can clearly see the small island with the church of Aghios Andreas, which in the old days also used to be the home of the monastery with the same name, before it was moved on shore for fear of pirate attacks. Next to the island of Aghios Andreas we can see the small group of isles called Diasporoi.

We return to Volimes and head towards the cape of Schinari and the Blue Cave. Along the way we come across the cute houses belonging to the settlement of Korithi, and drive past a small church by the road. We turn our attention to the inscription on its door which reads: "This is a Great Place, for it is none other than the House of the Lord and the Gate to

A church in Volimes

Heaven".

About 3 kilometres after Korithi we arrive at the promontory with the lighthouse which guards the edge of the land and warns passing ships at night. At the foot of this rocky shore we see the famous Blue Caves, created by continuous land erosion. The reflecting light inside these caves makes everything around them seem blue! The best time to visit these caves is early in the morning, when the light creates the

Picturesque grocery shop

159

strongest shades.

There are small boats that take visitors from the lighthouse to the caves, on a journey that takes 10 minutes either way. Boats also run the same trip from the harbour of Aghios Nikolaos, but whichever option you chose, don't forget to visit the Blue Caves before you leave the island.

After Korithi the road leads to the harbour of Aghios Nikolaos on the right. The isle of Aghios Nikolaos stands guard at the entrance to this small harbour. We can also see the ruins of the monastery of Aghios Nikolaos on the isle. Its beach, with small pebbles and rocks, manages to attract quite a few people who like swimming in the crystal-clear waters on this side of the island and enjoy visiting its caves. In fact, during the summer months, the beach road is practically overflowing with life as people flock the local sea-side taverns. Aghios Nikolaos also has a ferry connection with the island of Kefallonia during the summer season.

We follow the route which in about 3 kilometres will take us to our next stop, Makrys Gialos. Just before we reach this village, on our right we come across the intersection leading to the settlement of Askos. The road to the coast descends gradually and along most of the way we are offered a view of the sea and the Small Island or Mikro Nisi directly opposite.

Reflections in the Blue Caves

The beach of Makrys Gialos

The beach at Makrys Gialos extends on out left and features a pebble shore and crystal-clear waters. Even though this is one of the smaller beaches on the island, its wild beauty makes it one of the most beguiling. The rocks on its right-hand-side have been eroded into caves which can be reached by confident swimmers or by renting a canoe or pedalo. On the very top of the rock, which shelters the beach during the hottest hours of the day, a small tavern offers faithful campers a chance to enjoy good food and a great view of the beautiful area below.

On our way back to town we follow signs to Volimes and after passing through the village of Skinaria, we arrive at Ano Volimes. As we cut across the vineyards we notice the colourful ribbons, which the villagers tie on their plants to scare birds off, and are captivated by their movement to the shifting winds. As we leave the stone houses of the village behind, we drive through Volimes and onto the road that will take us back to Zakynthos.

A BOAT-TRIP AROUND THE ISLAND

Every morning around 9am, small boats set off from the port of Zakynthos on a journey around the island. There are a number of options available and cruises for every budget. Both the route and the stops for a swim along the way are basically the same, so all you have to do is pick the vessel you like the most.

Once out of the port, the boats follow a course which runs parallel to the island's north-western coastline. One of the most beautiful sections of the tour is at cape Schinari, when the boats approach the Blue Caves. Once past the promontory, the first stop is the famous Shipwreck, unless weather conditions dictate otherwise, in which case the captain usually comes up with an alternative suggestion. Stops along the coast usually last an hour, which is ample time to enjoy the sun and swim in the crystal-clear waters around the island. The next stop involves a visit to Porto Vromi. From that point onwards, the boats sail past the beaches and close to caves and ominous-looking rocky shores.

A short while before we reach the caves of Keri - this is usually the second stop for a swim and a visit to the impressive caves in the area - we sail past the cave of Papanikolis or "tou Papanikoli". They say that this is where the famous submarine was hiding during the Second World War. From the caves at Keri we sail towards the impressive rocks of Mizythra, on cape Marathias.

The boat sails across the gulf of Laganas and in front of the island of Marathonisi, on which we admire a beautiful beach. Boats usually slow-down between Marathonisi and Pelouzo, allowing passengers the chance to spot a Caretta-Caretta turtle if they are lucky.

Once past the cape of Gerakas we are offered a clear view of all the beautiful beaches along this coast. As we begin our final approach to the port of Zakynthos, I notice that it's almost 6pm.

A view of town and Bochali
The port

The famous Blue Caves

THE ISLANDS OF STROFADES

The small group of islands called Strofades, are situated 37 nautical miles south of the island of Zakynthos. During the summer season, there are daily connections to these by boat from town and Laganas.

The Strofades are comprised by the two islands of Arpina and Stamvranio, and their maximum altitude does not exceed 10 metres above sea-level, which is why they are also known as "Floating Islands", as they seem to float on the surface of the sea.

The name Strofades or Strofadia has its roots somewhere in the very distant past. Virgil associates the group's name with mythology: Voreos' two sons, Kalais and Zitis, were in pursuit of the mythological monsters known as Harpies, which the gods had sent to earth to punish humans and Phineus the soothsayer. However, when the monsters reached these islands and before they were captured by the two youths, Zeus ordered Voreos' suns to "turn back" ("strofi" in Greek means turn). Since then, the islands have been known as Strofades and the Harpies were able to build their nests in peace on these shores. Locals associate these mythological creatures to the birds of prey living on these islands, and which they nowadays call "artines".

In the 13th century on Arpina - the larger of the two islands and the only one to be inhabited - Erene the wife of the Byzantine Emperor Laskaris, built a monastery dedicated to the Transfiguration of our Savour and the Mother of God, the Spring of Eternal Joy. A church with the same name adorned by a marble icon-screen and a number of old icons, is situated on the tower's first floor. The monastery was frequented by

The monastery on Strofades

a number of saints, among which Aghios Dionysios, who later gave it his name.

In 1440, the monastery assumed its current form of a fortress-monastery, following the alterations executed by the emperor Ioannis Palaiologos. The island was subject to numerous attacks by pirates as well as invasions by barbarians, which led to the decision in 1717 to transfer the relics of Aghios Dionysios to Zakynthos. His empty grave lies in the temple of Aghios Georgios, on the ground floor of the monastery's tower. A 26-metre-tall tower dominates the scenery in front of the monastery.

The lighthouse guiding the passing ships by night, is situated on the northern side of the island.

TRADITIONAL ZAKYNTHIAN RECIPES
by Mrs Dionysia Pylarinos from the village of Orthonies

"Tsilipourdo"

(a dish for the evening of Easter Saturday made in the mountain villages in Zakynthos instead of the traditional Greek Easter tripe and herb soup called "mageiritsa")

The tsilipourdo is made by dicing the offal and intestines of a baby lamb or goat and then draining these. These are then boiled in a pot until they absorb their stock and are almost done.

As soon as they are almost ready, we add 1 glass of oil, some diced onion, 2 cloves of garlic, 2 bay leaves, 2 pieces of clove, some cinnamon and oregano. We may also add some diced tomato if we wish. Once we have added all the ingredients in the pot, we allow the mixture to cook on a low flame for 10' and then serve hot.

"Stuffed chicken"

Stuffed chicken or rabbit is one of the island's highly traditional recipes. Ask for it in the villages of Schiza and the other mountain villages across the island. However, one may also find this dish in certain taverns in town. Dice the offal of a chicken, add some diced potato and oily cheese, garlic cloves and salt and pepper to taste. We may also add some tomato if we wish. We place these in a small frying pan with some oil and brown until crispy. We use the mixture to stuff the thoroughly washed chicken and cut-off one of its wings, which we use to block the opening to the stomach and keep the stuffing inside. We carefully brown this in a frying pan with some oil and 1 glass of wine, and then let it cook on a low flame, adding fresh tomato juice and some water if necessary.

We prepare and stuff the rabbit in the same way, but we cook it without tomato juice and sew its stomach to keep the stuffing inside.

164

"Skordostoumbi Melitzana" (= Fried Aubergines in Garlic Sauce)

Skordostoumbi is one of the more common country recipes,

colander, once thoroughly salted. After about an hour, we fry them in very hot oil, remove them and keep them hot.

We grate a few tomatoes and boil them with some oil. As soon as the sauce is ready, we lay the slices of aubergine on a frying pan, add the sauce, some crushed garlic mixed with water, salt, pepper and oregano to taste, and cook for 10'.

Fried Cod in Garlic Sauce is also made in the same way. Once we have soaked the salt out of the cod over a period of a few days, we flour the cod and fry it, then lay on the frying pan, add the sauce prepared above, and cook for 10'.

"Beef Ragout"

A simple and very tasty Zakynthian country recipe, which Mrs Dionysia kindly prepared for us during our visit.

Brown some diced beef in oil. Once browned we add 1 glass of wine and let it cook until the wine evaporates. We then add some pepper, 1 bay leaf, some clove, oregano, 1 grated onion, 1 crushed garlic and some diced tomato.

We allow the mixture to boil on a low flame, occasionally adding some water if necessary.

In the past, but nowadays as well, in March the housewives would gather wild greens from the garden, along with white beet and poppy-greens with which they would prepare a tasty and simple dish called "Tsigaridia".

Once they cut the greens, they would boil these with fennel and fresh garlic. When ready, they would strain them and fry them in oil, tomato and pepper until they absorbed their stock.

as it is easy, cheap to make, and very tasty.

Cut a few slices of aubergine and soak the bitterness out of them by leaving them on a

Map of Zakynthos

ΧΕΛΩΝΕΣ CARETTA-CARETTA
CARETTA CARETTA TURTLES

Additional Information

INFORMATION

HOTELS

ZAKYNTHOS.....................0695
IRIA ....24682 B
OMONIA ....22113 B
STRADA MARINA ....22761 B
ALBA.............................26641 B
KRYONERI.......................28000 B
ZENITH ....22134 B
IONION ....22511 B
OLYMPIA ....28328 B
PHOENIX........................22419 C
PLAZA...........................28909 C
REPARO ....23578 C
TEREZA ....24500 C
ASTORIA ....835333 C
DIANA...........................28547 C
GARDELINO ....24333 C
ADRIANA ....28149 C
AEGLI ....28317 C
APOLO...........................42838 C
AVGI ....26641-2 C
ANGELIKA...............22391-28320
DIETHNES......................22286 C
DIZARO ....23644 C
DESSY............................28505 C
PALATINO ....45400 C
XENIA ....42666 C
ALIKES..............................0695
KOUKOUNARIA.................83533 C
ASTORIA ....83533 C
IONIAN STAR ....83416 C
MONTREAL ....83241 C
ALIKANAS........................0695
VALAIS..........................83223 B
VILLA SANTA MONICA ......83550 C
ARGASSI 0695
AKTI ZAKANTHA ....26441 A
CAPTAIN'S ....22779 A
CHRYSSI AKTI....................28679 B
LEVANTE ....22833 B
LOKANTA ....25563 B
MIMOZA BEACH ....22588 B
PALMYRA ....25707 B
ILIESA ....25346 B
ARGASSI BEACH ....28554 C
CASTELLO ....23520 C
COMMODORE ....26163 C
FAMILLY INN ....25359 C
BOCHALI 0695
AKROTIRI XENONAS ....28000 B
LOFOS STRANI................   B
VARRES..........................28352 B
KALAMAKI 0695
CAVO D'ORO ....22451 B
DANIEL...........................26094-5 B

DENNY'S INN ....27785 B
KALAMAKI BEACH ....22575 B
MERELEN ....26137 B
SIROKOS ....26088 B
VENUS...........................25611 B
LAGANAS 0695
ZANTE PARK....................51948 A
ASTIR............................51730 B
ESPERIA ....51505 B
GALAXY ....51171 B
LAGANAS ....51793 B
M.AEXANDROS..................51580 B
POSSIDON BEACH...........51199 B
VICTORIA ....51617 B
ZANTE BEACH ....51130 B
ZANTE HOTEL ....51611 B
ALKYONIS ....51194 C
ATLANTIS ....51142 C
AUSTRALIA ....51071 C
BLEU COAST ....51034 C
EVGENIA ....51149 C
ILIOS.............................51119 C
IONIS ....51141 C
OLYMPIA ....51644 C
SELINI...........................51154 C
SIRENE...........................51188 C
PLANOS............................0695
ST.DENIS ....25296 A
DIAS............................28105 B
MAVRIKIOS ....25907 B
MEDITERRANE ....26101 B
PARADISSOS ....45096 B
ALEXANDRA BEACH ....26190 C
ANETIS ....24590 C
COSMOPOLITE.................28752 C
OREA ELENI ....28788 C
TSILIVI ....23109 C
TRAGAKI...........................0695
CARAVELL II......................25261 A
PLAGOS BEACH ....24147 A
VASSILIKOS 0695
ZANTE ROYAL PALACE.....35493 A
AQUARIOUS.....................35300 B
LINA ....28531 B
XENIA ....22232 B
APOLLON ....22838 C
LIBRO D'ORO...................23785 C
VASSILIKON BEACH..........24114 C

CAMPING-SITES
ALYKES 83233
ZANTE CAMPING.............4475-61710
ANDREOLAS..................51585-51708
KREZIAS - "PARADISE" 61888
TARTARUGA 51967

REACHING ZAKYNTHOS

By air:
Olympic Airways has daily scheduled flights to Zakynthos all year long. The flight lasts about 45 minutes. The airport on Zakynthos is situated about 4 kilometres from town, in Ambelokipoi, and apart from domestic flights, also features a number of international flights from major cities around Europe. Visitors without private transport may travel on an Olympic Airways shuttle bus, which runs into town around departure times, or hire a taxi.

By sea:
The port of Kyllini, in the County of Ileia, is connected on a regular basis with Zakynthos. There are a number of ferry crossings every day and the journey lasts about an hour and fifteen minutes. For more information about departure times contact local agencies or the Co-operative of Zakynthian Cargo Vessels in Zakynthos (0695) 22083 and 48301, or Kyllini (0623) 92294 and 92422.
Miras Ferries: Zakynthos (0695) 48267, 41500
Kyllini (0623) 92100, 92080
Piraeus (01) 4174459, 4127225

By road:
There is a regular bus service that runs four-times daily from Athens to Zakynthos. The distance between Athens and the port of Kyllini is 286 kilometres and the drive takes around 4 hours and 30 minutes. For more information call the Public Transport Company in Athens (01) 5129 432, or Zakynthos (0695) 22255.

By rail:
There is a scheduled daily train service from Athens to the port of Kyllini. For more information call the Railway Company in Athens (01) 5131 601.

USEFUL TELEPHONE NUMBERS
Police: 22100
Town Hall: 22315
County Hall: 45195, 42792
General Hospital: 42514-5

Tourist Police: 42550
Port Authorities: 42417
Airport: 28322
Olympic Airways: 48611, 44433
Radio Taxis: 44724, 23623, 44036, 28261, 23788
Greek Telecom: 22139
Post Office: 42418

PETROL STATIONS
PETAS 42261
GOUSETIS.........................42157
PILARINOS 45532
KOTSONIS 45514
MALOUHOS 28524
GIANOULIS 42624
TSIMARA 48325
KLADIS 42869
THEODOSIS.......................24488
ZOUGRAS 28294
PLATIPODIS 51213
KAPNISIS............................48008
PAPADATOS 51832
SOULIS...............................46194
TSIPOS...............................49711
PILARINOS 43293
FIARAOS 61265
MILONAS...........................61207
KARATZAS 83478
VOUTOS.............................83246
POTHOS.............................61424
VOUTSOS...........................44687
MARGARIS 34289
DRAKOPOULOS 44688

PHARMACIES
MOUZAKIS 48238
VENETSANOU 23762
LEFTAKI..............................45284
MANESI 44061
ALIAZI 42403
HARTIS...............................22300
GIANIOTIS 23411
KLADI..................................27718
FRAGOGIANI......................44183
MOUZAKES.........................48238
VOUTOU..............................28462
ZARKADES.........................45044
PARASHI 27634
GAGOYDAKI.......................42623
VLADIANOU 23504
POMONI 42567
THEODOSI 26912
MANIOUDAKI 45466
SKAMNAKIS 42753
TOTA 45433
VITSIOS 28404

HIGH LIGHTS - INDEX

- Walking through town

- Visiting the temple of Aghios Dionysios in town

- Visiting Machairado and the temples of Aghios Timotheos and Aghia

Mavra

- Visiting museums and learning more about Ionian Art

- Walking to the Madonna Skopiotissa

- Swimming at the Shipwreck

- Visiting the Blue Caves

- Watching the sunset at Keri

- Walking through the island's wild natural surroundings

- Caring for the Caretta-Caretta turtle

- Buying local products (hand-woven products, honey, wine,

oil-cheese, mantolato (= traditional almond cakes), colognes)

- Savouring local recipes and tasting fine local wines to serenades

- Serenading

- Visiting the island in August (fetes, cultural events)

- Dressing-up for Carnival on the island

- Celebrating Easter on the island

FOOD & ENTERTAINMENT

Taverns throughout Zakynthos are famous for their serenading and the good food they offer their customers. Both in town, as well as in Kryoneri and Bochali, visitors will find a very wide range of restaurants and taverns to choose from, meeting all the requirements of international, Greek and local cuisine, and in most cases accompanied by traditional serenades.

If you have private transport, then we recommend you pick one of the fine taverns on the Lagoon at Keri for great fresh fish, or one of the local establishments at Vasilikos, famous for their traditional recipes and musical background. Then again, Aghios Nikolaos, Makrys Gialos, Kambi and Schiza, as well as almost any other village on the island boasts the capacity to offer visitors excellent local and international cuisine along with great hospitality and fine Zakynthian wine.

After dinner, for a somewhat different tone to your evening entertainment, we recommend you join the crowds at Argasi, Laganηs, Tsilivi and Alykes. These villages - and in many more villages around the island - one will find bars and night-clubs with excellent Greek and international music to satisfy every inclination and budget.

Οι πιο πρόσφατες
και πληρέστερες
εκδόσεις για το
νησί τη Ζακύνθου

300 παραδοσιακές συνταγές
Ελληνικής κουζίνας
σε μία πολυτελή έκδοση

BIBLIOGRAPHY

•"Zakynthos", Dinos Konomos, Kastrolofos and Aegiali, Part A, Volume I, Athens 1979

•"Grigorios Xenopoulos - Historic and Folklore Testimonies on Zakynthos", K. Papathanasis - Mousiopoulou, Athens 1988

•"Zakynthos in Greek and foreign poetry", Anthology by D. Serras, Athens 1994

•"The History of Zakynthos", Leonidas Ch. Zois, Athens 1955

•The Historic and Folklore Thesaurus of Zakynthos, Leonidas Ch. Zois, 1st Volume, Athens 1963

•"Zakynthian Architecture", Dionysios Zivas, Athens 1970

•"The Annals of Zakynthos", Dionysios Romas, The town of Zakynthos before and after the union to Greece, Athens 1964

•The Papyrus - Larousse - Britannica Encyclopaedia, Volume XXV, Athens 1984

•"Ionian Anthology", Athens 1934

•"Theatre on Zakynthos", D. Romas, "Theatre", Athens 1934

•"Churches and Monasteries on Zakynthos", Dinos Konomos, Athens 1967

•"Kathimerini", the newspaper, A Seven-day Feature on Zakynthos, 16/7/1995

•"Periplous", a Zakynthian magazine on literature and arts, published by D. Vitsos

ACKNOWLEDGEMENTS

The book in your possession would not have been written without the vital contribution of a number of people and local authorities, who were forthcoming with their help whenever necessary.

We wish to thank:

the Canon Alexios of the Cathedral in Zakynthos,
the manager and staff of the Municipal Library,
the manager of the Museum of Post-Byzantine Art,
the board of directors of the Museum of Solomos and Other Eminent Zakynthians,
and from the Municipal Hall in Zakynthos, Mr. Nikos Kefalinos and Mr. Takis Petropoulos for their invaluable help regarding the island's cultural events,
Mrs. Maria Loupa, responsible for County cultural events,
Mr. Takis Renesis,
the Pylarinos family from the village of Orthonies,
Mr. Giannis Piskardelis,

κάθε γωνιά της Ελλάδας ζωντανεύει στη...

GRECO card LTD

εκδοτική • τουριστική • διαφημιστική

Αγλαύρου 3, 117 41 Αθήνα, Τηλ.: (01) 9248292 / 293, Fax: (01) 9241910